12 Elephants and a Dragon

DR. VI TU BANH
with MARIE BESWICK ARTHUR

ISBNs:
eBook: 978-1-990688-27-0
Paperback: 978-1-990688-26-3
Audiobook: 978-1-990688-28-7

ABOUT THE PUBLISHER

Ingenium Books Publishing Inc.
Toronto, Ontario, Canada M6P 1Z2
ingeniumbooks.com

Edited by Boni Wagner-Stafford
Cover Design by Jessica Bell Design via Ingenium Books

PRAISE FOR *12 ELEPHANTS AND A DRAGON*

"An honest and heartfelt recount that feels like a harrowing distant tale and yet strangely familiar to all who had been refugees. One can only write this beautifully by one of two ways: through real lived experiences or spiritually channeled from the higher sources - the ancestors - and in this case, it's both."

—Nguyen Thien An, writer "Under the Squash Vines"

"A beautifully constructed memoir of an epic life journey. Vi Tu's story is nothing short of an odyssey with an underlying message of the power of good deeds, small moments of kindness, mentorship and perseverance."

—Dr. Carlye Jensen, President Uxbridge Health Center

"*12 Elephants and a Dragon* by Dr. Vi Tu Banh is a deeply moving and inspiring story of resilience, hope, and community. Through the lens of a young boy's journey from war-torn Vietnam to a new life in Canada, Dr. Banh beautifully captures the strength of the human spirit and the kindness of strangers.

This powerful memoir not only recounts the harrowing escape from Vietnam but also highlights the generosity of the Uxbridge families who helped them rebuild their lives. A must-read for anyone seeking a heartfelt tale of courage, survival, and the transformative power of compassion."

—Mayor Dave Barton, Uxbridge

"The story in this book is a saga told through the eyes of a boy who, through circumstance, had to grow up far too quickly and shoulder responsibilities far too grave for a child to bear. It is a compelling story of fear and generosity, failure and success, and the spirit of a young boy who grew into a pillar of the community which embraced his family.

That boy/man is the author, Vi Tu Banh. Vi Tu leads by example, always mindful of 'paying forward' and paying back the generosity extended by the community that welcomed his family in their time of greatest need.

Vi Tu is a Canadian who makes me proud of being born here. This is his story. It is a story that you must read. Reading it you will come to the realization that welcoming refugees is not an act of charity. Rather it is in our nation's self-interest."

—Michael McLuhan, Composer, Executor,
Estate of Marshall McLuhan

"In an epic journey across oceans and cultures, Vi Tu transports you into his immigrant family's story with vivid details. From embracing adult responsibilities while still a young boy, to realizing his vision of becoming a doctor, the thread of his Buddhist wisdom—gratitude, love, and compassion—is woven throughout, guiding him as he pays it forward to positively affect one billion people. An uplifting page turner!"

—Heidi Hackler, author
Food, Mood, Gratitude

"Dr. Vi Tu Banh's profound personal journey resonated deeply with me, both emotionally and spiritually. As a Vietnam war veteran, I felt compelled to assist the refugees known as 'Vietnam's Boat People' as they resettled in San Jose, California. The support from government programs was insufficient to help them build new lives; they needed direct, compassionate intervention. I rallied a group of fellow veterans and US Postal Employees who united to collect food, clothing, toys, and funds—filling the gaps where local governments fell short.

Dr. Banh's narrative, detailing his experiences and the incredible individuals who stood by him, serves as a powerful testament to the transformative power of love and service. I honor all those who dedicate themselves to uplifting humanity. This is a story that deserves to be shared—a message that should inspire countless others. Spread the word! Tell a dozen people."

—Reverend Bill McDonald, Vietnam vet, author, poet, speaker

"*12 Elephants and a Dragon* is a captivating account of a wounded boy's journey to becoming a healer for the community that provided him a home. Dr. Banh's narrative, filled with bravery and honesty, is a poignant memoir that features unforgettable voices, rich symbolism, and most importantly, lessons that are highly relevant in today's world. His story is a timely and necessary addition to the literary landscape."

—Dr. Jennifer Wilson, author
Grant Us Tomorrow: A Medical Memoir

"A moving true story about a young Vietnamese family of eight fleeing their war-ravaged homeland for the chance of freedom, the hardships they endured, their gripping resiliency, and remarkable courage. A must read to help us better understand the trials and tribulations of The Boat People who came to Canada."

—Gerri Lynn O'Connor, former Uxbridge mayor

CONTENTS

To Mom and Dad
我將此書呈獻予我最尊敬的父母。

FOREWORD

IN THE LATE 1970s, AFTER reading news reports and seeing pictures of the horrendous plight of the Vietnamese refugees—the boat people—my husband and I embraced the opportunity to become involved. We joined a group of like-minded Uxbridge residents and, in cooperation with the Canadian government's initiative, we readied for the arrival of our family.

A generous Uxbridge resident offered a house rent-free; we put out a call for, and collected, donations of clothes, household essentials, and toys.

Each member of the group accepted a specific role: health care, education, immigration, employment, and shopping. We were well prepared.

What I wasn't prepared for was the emotional impact of that first meeting at the airport. I saw a dad, a pregnant mom, and six young children looking weary, confused, and apprehensive. Within moments, they were no longer nameless, faceless boat people; they were a family, not unlike my own.

They wore Canadian hand-me-downs. They appeared empty-handed—they had nothing.

It didn't take me long to realize I was wrong. They had everything they needed: intelligence, ambition, motivation, trust, and a willingness to do whatever it would take to survive and succeed. The parents set an example and accepted jobs the rest of us were reluctant to do. The kids delivered newspapers, plucked chickens, picked berries, shoveled snow, and worked hard at school. Each of the children, now grown, has a postsecondary education, is an outstanding professional, and is a valuable contributor in their respective communities. Two have returned to live in Uxbridge and are active and generous participants in all aspects of life in our community. They all have reasons to be proud of what they have accomplished. I consider myself fortunate to have travelled this road with them.

—Barbara Murphy, 2023
(ninety-seven years old and the only living
sponsor at time of writing)

Chapter 1

The Courage

Once upon a true time, there was a boy who lived in an extraordinary story that contained temples, an old boat on a treacherous ocean, tropical islands, and treasure. In the backdrop of the story were weapons, war, and heartbreaking goodbyes. But the boy was carried by resilience and enduring spirit.

The boy mostly kept the story inside his heart, occasionally releasing bite-size pieces. But the story couldn't remain locked in his heart, for there was the promise he made to his father to tell it in full.

The duty to tell the story was sometimes so powerful that the boy could not sleep through the night—even when he pushed the promise under the pillow. When he did sleep, the story flooded his dreams. Promise and story became a relentless duo, present when the boy was busy figuring out how to do things that children do—and while overreaching himself in schoolwork, and jobs before and after school.

When the boy became a man, he became preoccupied with further education, becoming an eye doctor, establishing a practice, and making a difference in the world. Even after a life-changing adventure of spirit from which the man regrouped and began to set down some notes, telling his story gave way to more pressing matters.

Over time, the boy inside the man became smaller and smaller. From time to time, the boy wandered into the den, disturbing the dust on the notes and files.

Sometimes, when the man was in the living room, directly below the den, the boy would knock over a book. But the man did not hear it fall, nor did he notice it on the floor the next time he was in that room.

Powerless to get the man's attention, the boy wept when the den was packed up and moved to another home—the man might never unseal the boxes.

With the material out of sight, the boy inside the man began narrating the story while the man slept. Several times a month, the boy inside the man simply asked for the story to be told.

Every time the boy asked, the answer was the same.

"Not now, Boy, not yet. I have a business to run, causes to support, dreams to fulfill, and pay-it-forwards to complete."

Over and over, the boy quietly accepted the answer.

Then, one day, the boy woke earlier than the man. He sat on the bottom of the bed and watched the man rise. He followed him into the bathroom while the man brushed his teeth.

When the man padded down the hallway toward the kitchen, the boy was already sitting at the table. "SIR, IT IS TIME—" the boy called out.

"Not now, Bo—" The man recoiled as he entered the kitchen. At his table sat a dragon.

The dragon breathed out swirls of fire that sizzled into the rough ocean that had appeared in a stormy reality around the table.

The man gripped the back of his chair, managed to sit, then rubbed his eyes.

When the man refocused, the turbulent sea flowed away, but the majestic creature with the boy's voice remained. "Sir, the world is ready for our story."

The man caught his breath. Ten thousand memories flooded him—market stalls, one after the other, laden with goods and offering services, the pungent and comforting aroma of pho, the ocean and—bodies—so many bodies . . .

"Okay, Boy. Lead the way," said the man.

Chapter 2

Three Million Steps

Perhaps it was stubbornness
or determination
that stopped my grandfather
from seeing the writing on the wall,
or his optimism clouded reality.
It may well have been fear from the souls
who did not believe
their lives could be obliterated.

My grandfather's feet were the base of a tree of his knowledge, his toes curved as if they would root into the dusty ground—if he ever stopped walking. When I was four, I thought he was a thousand years old. Sometimes, when we were squatting to eat, for then we were almost eye-to-eye, I wondered if it would be possible to count the rings of him, like a tree, but then I'd get lost on one of the roads of his wrinkles, and inside one of his stories.

It was on our walks and over bowls of rice that he filled me with the past.

"Vi Tu," he said. "You almost had no age." He explained that my mother had been ill during her pregnancy with me and that my grandmothers—from both sides—separately visited an oracle at two different temples for their help for my mother's health so that she may deliver a healthy child. Each oracle told my grandmothers that there was a message from my paternal uncle who had died as a child. "Let me take care of the boy," said the spirit of my uncle. The deal was that I be given over to my grandfather.

When my parents agreed, my mother instantly became well.

I was not the first grandchild, but by default—because my father worked with my grandfather—I was treated as the first. I was a boy: the golden one for my grandfather. Despite that, I always felt my uncle's presence and came to regard his spirit as an adopted father from another realm.

Grandfather's stories were delivered to me as leaves falling from an ancient dầu tree—one or two drifting down in a quiet time, or a series rushing by as if the wind had whipped around a branch at the end of a season and threatened to scatter them should someone not gather them for safe-keeping. There was always a sense of purpose with his stories; they must be kept preserved, leaves pressed between pages, to hold together the promise of the cycle of life.

From the time I could speak, my life revolved around the compound my grandfather had created for my family and some extended family, and the market. It was hard to know where one family started and the other began, so enmeshed were my parents and grandparents and a handful of relatives— separate dwellings in one compound. Each house was part business—workshop, cutting room, sewing room, store—and part living area.

There were windows—without glass, because that was the norm. The tropical, humid climate required ventilation, and fans were always turned on. Some days, I'd have three showers. Behind our closed doors and open windows, we spoke a dialect of Chinese called Hakka. The centre of each home was the kitchen, where we were taught to sit up straight and use our chopsticks properly, never pointing them when we spoke. Despite the formality, a chicken or three often walked around parts of the house. We did not have any other animals, but other families in our community used dogs to protect their property; I was terrified of those dogs. While my brothers and sisters would walk around barefooted, I'd wear slippers or sandals for the purpose of having something to kick or throw at any dog that chased me.

I went with my grandfather to the Cho Bến Thành market every day, sheltered under his success. One day, I became separated from my grandfather. Lost and overwhelmed, I stood screaming and crying. "You were never lost, and not alone for long," he told me when we were reunited.

"Not long is forever for me, Grandfather," I told him.

One day, on the way to the market, he asked, "Vi Tu, do you see that street vendor over there?"

"The poor man?" I asked.

My grandfather's footfalls became heavy with disappointment. "Vi Tu, you are looking at your history. I was that man. Your grandmother and I survived by selling what we could. Then we learned to sew. Our clothing store in our family compound and our stall in the biggest market in the world rose from that past," he said.

"I'm sorry, Grandfather." We hurried to avoid pull carts, bicycles, motorcycles, and little cars that looked like big bugs in the massive circle of traffic that circled in front of Bến Thành. His steps were still heavy.

"Honourable people have been selling their wares by the Saigon River for as long as anyone can recall. No one is any less than another. No one is 'just a vendor' or 'just a teacher' or 'just a son.' Each person brings value to the whole. Never say you are 'just,' Vi Tu. Value others as you wish to be valued yourself." He then quoted Lao Tzu, as he often did: *You can mould clay into a vessel, yet it is its emptiness that makes it useful.*

My grandfather's storytelling pace resumed; he'd forgiven my judgement of the poor street vendor. "Your father was the fifth child of our twelve children. But it was your father who agreed to work with me in the trade, so in the way of honour, it was like he was my first. He may not always be happy about this choice, and he may rant about how it caused a rift between the siblings, but it is how you became my golden child—the first son of the first son. That is a privilege and a responsibility." His steps became lighter as they traced the route of millions of traders toward the marketplace.

He liked to share before-we-were-born stories. He told me he was married to my grandmother before either one of them was on the Earth because their parents had arranged their marriage. When my father was a teenager, my grandparents had done much the same: found a wife for him who would work in the family business.

"It requires hard work to set up a home, Vi Tu. And it takes determination and courage to leave that home," he said. He stopped walking, found a twig on the side of the road, and drew a rudimentary map of China in the dust at our feet. "When your grandmother and I were in our twenties, we lived here, in Guangzhou." "Day after day, we heard about the brutality of the Japanese forces occupying Manchuria north of us. I wished we could fly south, like the birds, but we could not. So we walked."

He told me how he and my grandmother fled China in the 1930s by walking from China to Vietnam. Not just to the northern border, but all the way to Saigon. They walked.

I looked in an atlas and measured the distance: 1,500 miles by road. Distances meant little to me, a young boy who rarely walked farther than to and from the market. But numbers were everything.

I slid the beads of my abacus, my first toy, along the horizontal rows of wire and counted, calculated, and computed my way through hundreds of hypothetical equations. I worked out that my grandparents put one foot in front of the other more than 3,700,000 times.

Chapter 3

Pride and Ridicule

I DREADED GOING TO SCHOOL. I wouldn't have gone if it weren't for the nanny my grandparents had arranged to take me and pick me up. Outside the school, other children would point their fingers to my head with one of their hands as a gun, then they would mimic pulling the trigger while shouting, "BANH!" To them, my name in Vietnamese sounded like the blast of a gun. So did the translation to Cantonese: "PANG!" Soon their gestures escalated into physical assaults. In Chinese culture, a person's last name is their seal of approval. My grandfather and father were proud of their names but, for me, our last name was a source of ridicule.

In the safety of the classroom, the bullies were unable to attack me. We sat in rows of ten students with as many as a hundred in each class. We learned math on an abacus—my favourite. Strict by design, there was punishment for speaking—consequences included either standing in the corner or being whipped in front of the class.

There was always a challenge to take on or a contest to enter. Calligraphy and speed-writing—the fastest and neatest wins a prize. As well as math and logic, hard work and perseverance were my strengths. I often took first place.

Still, the bullies meant I couldn't wait for the school day to end so I could get back to my job at the market. My grandfather continued to teach me about karma, explaining that giving and service is done with no expectation of return—the returning takes care of itself. "Uphold the honour of our name: Banh," he said.

I shivered at the sound of it.

Between school and my duties in the business, there was little downtime. Except for chess. I moved my chess piece but did not remove my fingers from it. My grandfather frowned. I pulled it back and chose another move. He smiled.

"This is my favourite time of day," I said. "Chess-playing time."

"We are not playing." He considered his move. "You are learning the business."

"But there are no patterns here," I said, looking around.

"There are patterns everywhere," he said.

"Chess is not clothing," I said.

"Strategy is necessary for success in everything," he said, and he moved his bishop. "Especially business. When you were one month old, I took over an entire restaurant and celebrated you. You will continue to grow the business your grandmother and I built."

He made his move. I quickly made mine.

He frowned. "Patience is also important. Check."

I put my head in my hands. He had won again. His hand found my hair and ruffled it. By the time I brought myself to study the board, he was standing.

"Is it still your favourite time of day?" he asked.

And then it was time for me to smile. I had seen my mistake, and I rearranged the pieces to help me remember what I had done.

"You will do well when you take over the business," he said.

It seemed an impossibly long time before I would take over anything. "Thank you for the chess," I said to my grandfather. We were in the main office room in my grandparents' section of the house. "I'll get ready to leave with Auntie."

"We are doing well," he said. "We share our success with others, and that brings more treasure for the heart. Karma blesses us with health and with the money we receive from sales." He looked toward the giant black box that was anchored in the corner of the main room. "Our life's savings are inside that safe," he said.

"It is a successful business, Grandfather." I wasn't sure whether to be grateful or afraid of the huge box that seemed to have a life of its own.

"Go sell to your Americans," he said.

Our best customers were American soldiers. My grandfather had thought of the idea of changing some of the patterns of the clothing we made to fit the larger, muscled bodies of those soldiers.

"They have the money to purchase tailored shirts any time they are on leave," he said.

"On leave from what?" I asked. I never got an answer.

Our market stall received a steady flow of American military and the cash that came with it—many of them found a way to say that they had heard of us from other soldiers who were pleased with the clothing we made. Most days, I sold shirts to them, calculating the prices on my abacus and putting the cash into a money box to be later transferred to the big, black safe.

Money from that safe fed our family, and it helped many others. People came to Grandfather for help, and he assisted. He answered many questions that others brought to him about business and life.

Chapter 4

My Hidden Father

IN THE MORNING, I WOULD see my father sewing with the employees. I'd go to school, and when I came home, he'd still be sewing. But sometimes, without warning, he'd spring to his feet and head up to the attic. He'd stay there a long time: hours, or sometimes even days. This went on through one year, then into the next, and—since I was pretty good at math, I knew exactly how long this went on—for six years he stayed inside our home except the occasional time when my uncle, a police officer, took him out on his motorcycle.

One time, after he and my uncle returned, I heard my father say that they'd had a close call. Some government officials had stopped them. He told my mother that my uncle had said he was transporting my father on police business, and so they were permitted to carry on. After that, I noticed my uncle didn't take my father out again. He visited us less often too. When he did visit, I heard whispers of war. I heard phrases like, "The north is continuing its invasion," or "The south will fall to Hồ Chí Minh's army," and "How long will the Americans stay?"

My brothers and sisters—another one born every year, for a time—grew up with it as a normal part of life. My mother and my grandmother chatted with each other about recipes and children's behaviour in a mostly happy way. They cooked. They sewed. My mother had babies. But we did not speak about my father's behaviour.

Meanwhile, each of our days were like any other. We worked in the family business, the thread becoming wet between the tailors' fingers, sewing machines chugging through the thick and heavy air of the compound. Over time, those days included my mother jumping at every loud sound, and my grandmother looking over her shoulder a lot. When my aunt and I went to the market, she was not as bubbly. There were fewer American soldiers buying shirts. Grandfather told fewer stories.

"Saigon is falling," said a passing teenager when I escaped to the street for a break from my duties. "Have you not heard the explosions?"

I wasn't sure if I had or that I didn't want to.

"What of the helicopters?" said the teenager. "Our people are trying to get onto American helicopters to escape torture and death here. My father says that life as we know it will no longer exist."

I retreated to the safety of our compound. My family was sewing. Nothing had changed. The chickens were in the kitchen, the rice was on the stove, there were bolts of fabric waiting to be cut. The sewing machines were still singing their song of our family enterprise. What did that stupid teenager know?

Days later, officials arrived at our door. I was tucked away with the other children while my grandparents represented the family. But I watched the North Vietnamese soldiers come into our compound and haul away the huge black box that stood in the corner of the office. It took several of them to lift all our treasures and load our life's savings into a truck and drive away.

"We all work for Hồ Chí Minh now," said one of the workers from our compound.

"Hồ Chí Minh died in 1969," said another.

"Hồ Chí Minh is eternal. Now there is one Vietnam," said the first.

"Millions will die," said my mother.

"Millions have died," said my father.

"You won't die," said my mother to my father. "The South will no longer need their people to be soldiers."

I looked to my grandfather, confident he would help me make sense of what was happening. Surely, my grandfather would not let anything else bad happen. He was the head of our family and a community leader. He had made something from nothing, and he could do it again.

"There will be no more private school, Vi Tu," my grandfather said.

"But, Grandfather, you built that school," I said.

He nodded and looked at his feet, as though searching them for the peace he used to hold within himself.

In that instant, the war I hadn't known was happening was over. No one had told me my American customers had been on leave from the battlefields. At night, I'd lie on my low bed not knowing whether to be scared or excited about the future. Outside, there'd be only the howl of a dog, the clang of a garbage can, and an occasional song from someone who remembered how to soothe a bad dream.

I hadn't realized that the absence of gunfire was a sound.

Chapter 5

The Year of the Dragon

April 1975 had signalled the Fall of Saigon. Not long after, all around the marketplace hung signs that said I lived in the Socialist Republic of Vietnam in the city of Hồ Chí Minh.

I quietly welcomed the Year of the Dragon, on what the western world called January 31, 1976. Aptly, it was a fire dragon. And why not? The world as I knew it might as well have been scorched earth. I pieced together a quilt of my own understanding that ours was no longer a family business. We worked for someone named Hồ Chí Minh, who was dead but whose followers had become an extension of his vision for Vietnam.

My grandfather stared at the space where the safe used to be. He said nothing. I avoided his dark mood.

Sporadic gunfire sounded in the distance.

"Resisters," said my mother.

"That is what the whole country has been hearing for decades," said one of the workers.

"Sew," said my father to the worker.

My father went outside a lot more. His mood was brighter. Still, he had his low moments. Sometimes, at night, I heard him speak about his frustration that my grandfather had gotten us all into a difficult situation by making him have too many children to work in the family business. He said he'd been painted into a corner. Now what would he do? He railed on about his siblings and their other careers, how some had returned to China and others lived in Hong Kong. Was he speaking to the moon?

I heard people in our community talking about a surrender speech they'd heard on the radio.

"We are officially Hồ Chí Minh City," they said.

"What does that mean?" I asked.

"It means you must never say Saigon again," they said.

I struggled to understand all the things I was hearing. My abacus was of no help to me in learning what was happening. People were fleeing Saigon, no, Hồ Chí Minh City. Hundreds of thousands had been bribed with rice in exchange for their promise to leave the city to farm in the countryside. Others had been placed in reeducation camps that were not really for learning but for torture, disease, hard labour, and death.

"Vi Tu," said my grandfather. "Your grandmother and I are returning to China. We will be going to Hong Kong."

The black cloud over his head told me all I needed to know. I would not be going with him.

"Has someone given you a bowl of rice?" I asked.

CHAPTER 6

A Thousand Cuts

SUDDENLY, IT WAS THE YEAR of the Snake. There were no fresh footsteps in which to place my own feet. My grandfather's sandals were no longer by the door; his baggy jacket did not hang nearby. He travelled to Hong Kong with my grandmother late in 1977.

We sewed through the Year of the Horse, 1978. The community I lived in had changed from a place of hardworking, carefree simplicity to one filled with whispers about the evil government and who was the latest victim of its persecution. So much impending doom. I walked from space to space in our compound as if looking for a left-behind book. The chessboard gathered dust, the wet kind that doesn't blow away. Even the chickens stopped clucking.

"They aren't our chickens anymore," someone said to me one day when I chased a hen away from a stack of fabric. Running my hand over the bright cotton, I looked to the workroom, where the hands of family members were seaming clothing together. I thought it odd that not even the smallest stitch on the straightest line was ours. A power greater than all of us had taken away the essence of our family: our family business. I sat in a corner and, for the first time since I could remember, I did absolutely nothing.

"Get up," said my father. "There is work to be done."

The hardened jaw I saw in his expressions caused a shiver down my spine. I rose. "Yes, Father." As I followed him out of the room, he appeared taller.

My grandparents wrote that they had arrived in China, along with tens of thousands of others. Ink on paper through which I could see the dark clouds of my mentor's mood.

Sometimes I'd see my mother and father huddled in private conversation. When they did this, they glanced out the glass-less windows, lowering their voices, pausing if someone was nearby. They even stopped speaking if they knew I was near. We were working for Hồ Chí Minh. We didn't have our own business but ran it for the Republic. If we did what we were told to do, nothing horrible would happen.

My parents' whispers concerned me.

Sometimes my thoughts moved to places so fearful that my dreams were filled with scenarios in which my parents were taken away by authorities. Or the eldest child's scariest nightmare: me running the business, going to school, taking care of all my siblings, and running the house. I'd calm myself with the knowledge that we no longer owned the business and there was no longer a school like the one I'd attended. Still, there were all those siblings to care for: five of them.

My father's strong voice and his leadership came at our family life like parallel railway tracks. He'd bitterly curse about his lot in life, yet he spoke with a louder voice and was more involved than ever with the goings-on. When the Horse galloped out of the Chinese calendar and the Goat appeared in 1979, my father seemed even taller.

He had rarely mentioned his siblings—and only then in negative terms—but after Grandfather left, in my father's emerging strength, there was a kind of soft mattress in the corner of his conversations about his brothers. Suddenly, he didn't appear brotherless, and I did not feel uncle-less.

Father began to speak about a brother who had gone to Australia in a boat. My mother would nod and say a few words about how good it would be for my uncle and his family to feel freedom. My father would nod to my mother. Then they would take their discussion to another room.

Workers and neighbours shared stories of others who had left—like my uncle had. Horror stories. I walked away from them with pictures in my head of people in Vietnamese jails or in boats turned upside down by huge waves. My father would not walk away from those stories; he would confront the storyteller and downplay the danger or up-play the importance of freedom. "That is a small proportion." "Independence has a price." "Maybe it is better to perish than to remain in Vietnam." "It worked for my brother."

My mother would nod in his direction. He was the leader of our family. She was his right hand. They were a team. The black safe was gone. But I saw my father look over his shoulder when income was accounted for. I did not question him but wondered why he seemed so nervous about the accounting.

Then my father's eldest brother died of colon cancer. The chronological first son, who had been replaced by my father, the fifth, was gone. My father gathered us and the families together and spoke as a leader. He spoke of karma and how we needed a lot of the good kind.

Then came word that two of my father's nephews had tried to leave Vietnam. One had been shot and bled to death. "So fearful are they of the government, no one will claim my nephew's body. Even his own father," said my father to my mother. "And so I will."

He went by himself. I retreated into deep thoughts when he was gone. I told myself over and over that he'd return. I could not picture how my cousin had been shot or what he looked like. I only knew what physical death looked like on chickens.

I sat and unlocked the vault of the stories my grandfather had told me about death when he'd talked about Taoism and Buddhism. Death, to my child mind, was simply a door, because my grandfather had said it was so. An invitation to another energy.

My father claimed my cousin's body. He received a visit from his brother, who bowed to my father. It was as if my father had sewn the estranged family back into a sibling group using a magic needle and golden thread.

Chapter 7

Hope

THE COMPOUND, THE BUSINESS, THE chickens, the chairs—
not even the cooking pots were ours. What had been so
terrible suddenly seemed okay—if only for the fact that my
parents stopped complaining about being "owned by the
government." Instead, they whispered, and some of their
whispers drifted to me. They wanted to leave Vietnam. We
might leave. There was a dream. There was hope.

The sun rose. I rolled over.

"Get dressed," said my father. He never told me to get
dressed. "Wear several layers of clothing."

I opened my eyes. Had I heard him right? I pointed out it
was already hot and would be even hotter later.

"Now," said my father. "Shorts over shorts over shorts.
Shirts over shirts over shirts. "Gather your brothers and
sisters. Make sure they wear many sets of clothing too."

He told me if we had some small things we wanted to carry, we could. If they were small.

I did what I was told, at least in part. I got my siblings dressed and ready—but I had to bring a big thing, not a small one. Responsibility. It was all I could carry anyway, as my hands were needed to corral, hold, grab, and supervise my youngest siblings. We walked to a cube truck that I recognized as one used for transporting ice. My mother had a small bag, the kind she used to take to market. We stood looking up at the back of the ice truck. Then a man came around to where we all were, unhooked a metal latch, and hoisted up the rolling door. Cold air rushed out like a fast-flowing river. It was such a relief to have the heat of the day stripped away.

"Hurry," said the man.

"Quick, Vi Tu," said my father.

It seemed we were propelled up and into a frozen, dark reality. There were canvas panels on blocks of ice as well as more to take the chill off our bodies.

"Sit," said the man as he tugged down the metal rolling door.

I regretted my earlier relief from the heat. I could not stop shivering.

A line of Chinese characters typed across my brain to represent the 30th day of March, 1979. The day I left the place I was not allowed to call Saigon.

Chapter 8

Escape in the Year of the Dragon

"Father, what is happening?" I asked several times, as the ice truck bumped down the road.

"The less you know, the better," he said.

"But I can help if I know," I said.

He sighed in the dark, only the tiniest shafts of light poking in from the edges of the rolling door. "This ice truck will deliver us to a place where we'll board a boat. I've paid for our passage in gold—all eight of us."

He described a big boat. A safe boat. One that could comfortably accommodate a lot of people.

"And the boat will take us to . . . where?" I asked. I'd never been outside the city before.

My father did not answer.

We travelled for a day and a half, huddled in the back of the ice truck, heading south toward the ocean. My father adjusted the waistband of his shorts many times. Were they too big? My mother tended the youngest children. I tried to keep the older of my younger siblings settled on the canvas cloth that did a poor job of insulating us from the top of the ice. I tried to get my brothers and sisters to eat a little rice. Their lack of appetite mirrored mine.

We got out of the truck on April 1, 1979. Landing on the ground after sitting for so long sent shockwaves through my legs, but there was no time to complain. My father motioned for us to leave the truck quickly.

"This place is Cà Mau," my father said to my mother. "From here, we will go to freedom." I wondered where this placed called Freedom was—and how long it would take us to get there.

No matter what direction I looked, the stench of fish assaulted me. We were on a street with buildings on one side and a curved harbour on the other. It was as though a giant had taken a cleaver to the land, carving out a hole for the sea to fill in. While the water was calm and nothing like I'd heard in the horror stories about others who had tried to escape to Freedom, the harbour was crowded. It was like a parking lot full of boats. I tried to picture how the large craft my father had described, the one that would take us to Freedom, would get into the harbour. It didn't look like there was enough space.

The streets that led away from the harbour contained stalls, little buildings, and a large Buddhist temple. My father turned to me and pointed to the temple. "We sleep in there," he said.

"Is our boat not coming?" I asked.

My father pointed to two boats anchored side by side in the grey water. "When the captain says the time is right, we'll board one of those two boats."

"But, Father," I said. "Those do not look like big boats to me."

He turned away. I followed him to the sanctuary that would be a temporary home. We slept on the temple's floor, which provided relief from the tropical heat of Cà Mau but didn't make me shiver like I had in the ice truck.

The next day, the captain explained that based on Feng Shui, the time was still not right.

For seven nights we slept on the cool floor, and for seven days we blended into the crowds of the city. I felt like we were fugitives, like we were traitors to our new Republic.

Yet no officials stopped us.

"The officials are paid to look the other way," said my father. "By those who arrange all the departures." My father exchanged looks with my mother. The streets around the port buzzed with the electricity of escape. I stared at the harbour, blending my skills with the abacus and on the chessboard, but no matter how many hypothetical calculations and permutations I tried, I just couldn't fit all the people around us into all the boats in the harbour, let alone two. And then word reached us. It was time for the hordes of us to leave.

"Help your mother with the children," said my father.

The nearer I got to the boats, the larger they seemed. And then, up close, I could see that the fresh paint had been painted over rough old boards.

I imagined the boats speaking to us as we filed on. "I'm sorry," they said. "You were lied to."

"It's not your fault," I whispered. "You are boats, not people."

On the slow walk to Freedom—or death—I learned that our captain and the family that owned both boats were also fleeing Vietnam. They were risking their lives just as we were, but their pockets were filled with our gold. I looked to my father, fiddling again with his waistband, and wondered if he felt he had been taken advantage of. All that gold! My grandfather's black mood entered me.

The boats rocked; if they hadn't been tethered, I think they would have made a deal with the wind to take them away from all of us. My father knew how many shirts could be cut from a bolt of fabric. That knowledge should have told him that by the same kind of calculation "this" many people could not fit on "these" boats.

But he had paid. I saw defeat and hope compete in his expression. Eventually, responsibility wiped out both, and he encouraged us to buy in.

My father had been living on hope, and he had been feeding it to us. It might be all we had to eat before we were swallowed by the ocean. Unless we were not. In that final moment of private thought before going shoulder to shoulder with hundreds of others, I vowed to leave behind the cloud of my grandfather's crushing defeat as well as my former country. This harbour would be the start to my new life.

Chapter 9

4581 and 4518

I LOST COUNT OF THE people boarding after 250. I padded behind my family up a plank onto the deck of the smaller of the two boats my father had pointed to, all those days ago, from shore. Painted in black on the bow were the numbers 4581. Across from us was the larger of the twin boats, wearing 4518.

As I stepped onto 4581, then down some stairs under the deck, I felt the squishiness of rotting timber under my feet. There were rows of long, thin boards we were to sit on. The conditions below decks broke my heart a little bit, and then my father's expression broke it a little bit more. I sat with my brothers and sisters between my parents on a small section of a bench, but the stream of people kept coming. Our space was disappearing. My younger siblings were squeezed out of their spots like they were in a vice and had to sit on each other's laps.

I multiplied benches by people by rows. There were over 300 of us on this boat, which I estimated was about sixty feet long.

The captain gave the order to untie from the mooring, even as thumps of bodies hitting the deck above me sounded. People from shore, desperate to leave Vietnam, were leaping onto the boat—opportunity seizing them or them seizing it, I was not sure. My father had been right: My uncle could have joined us.

I looked around at dozens of families clustered in tight knots of hope and fear. Not a murmur among us, packed like sardines, sitting below decks, on the floor, on benches row-by-row, facing each other, backs to each other, side by squished side.

Human cargo.

We left at night, obeying the command not to speak a word, but our departure was anything but silent. *Boom-grind-rattle-chug.* My brothers and sisters covered their ears.

Peering through a crack in the hull, I saw that our over-full boats, 4518 and 4581, were being escorted out of the bay by boats and men in uniforms.

"They've been bribed to permit the exit," said a passenger near us.

Perhaps they were the same officers who had ignored all the new people in the port city. Maybe their wives or sisters or brothers had food stalls and welcomed the extra money that came to their business. Possibly they were overwhelmed by how difficult it would be to enforce the rules, so they took money instead and looked to their own horizon.

I did some more calculations. The weight of all the people on our boat was surely too much for its size.

Chapter 10

Directionless

THE ENGINE CONTINUED TO ROAR, an echo from the other boat nearby.

The sea below us was calm at first. "We're not really at sea," said a passenger. "This is the harbour."

The cool wind swirled from up on the deck and provided some air in the thick breaths of all the people below. It was good to inhale more than each other's fear. Then my body jerked forward. The bench I was on, and all the people on it including me, rose at one end, as if it were jumping a fence. That end dropped and the previously lowered end rose.

"Now we're out of the harbour," said that same passenger.

The world changed to a wild ride. I squeezed out from between my family, clambered up on deck, and made my way to the captain, who appeared less official than his title. He wore shorts and a frayed shirt, had the weathered skin of someone who has spent a lot of life in the elements, and he carried himself like he had taken more orders than given them.

"Where are we going?" I asked him in Chinese.

"I do not know," he replied.

I switched to Vietnamese. "You do not know?" The wind stole my words; my eyes stung from the sea's spray.

His gnarled hand hovered over the compass, the tip of a dirty finger near a squiggly symbol at its base. I knew some letters of the English alphabet and recognized the S for south. I pictured a page of an atlas I'd seen at school. The blue ocean on that illustration was nowhere in sight. We were on a turbulent nightmare of gunmetal grey. Either he didn't have time for me, or he really didn't know where we'd end up, just that we were going south.

As I returned below decks, I passed a narrow door I hadn't noticed before on my way back to my parents. It was slightly open, and there was a kind of tube with a hole. A wall of stench hit me. My stomach lurched as I realized it was the toilet. One. For 300 of us.

I swallowed, then squeezed back into the cluster of my family.

A full night of tossing and bucking gave way to the intense heat and humidity of daytime. Vomit was everywhere. There was no water to drink. People began dropping from dehydration. When they lost consciousness, they wouldn't fall to the ground, just onto the person next to them. Some even remained erect because they were held up by a tight line of bodies.

Broken rows of humans on a broken boat, I thought.

Someone screamed. A powerful stream of seawater poured into the boat through a hole. Every time we hit a strong wave, which was almost every few seconds, more water would rush in through it.

"We'll all go down," someone said.

I watched another passenger ball up a piece of cloth from his own possessions and stuff it into the hole. Water leaked in around it, but it held—until the next wave.

"The hole is not new. It's been patched before," he said.

"There are more," said someone else.

"Please, 4581, please take us to somewhere light and safe," I prayed.

When there was a steady crew of re-patchers and patching material, I took my attention to the bathroom behind the engine room—or the door to it. The was a constant revolving line of people waiting, going in, coming out. So many of us. One bathroom. Even if there had been someplace to wash hands after using the bathroom, which there wasn't, the sea state would have rendered it impossible. I vowed not to use the bathroom at all until we were off the boat.

Chapter 11

Futility

By DAY THREE, MY MIND drifted in and out of wishing. One moment I'd see the water level through a porthole, the next I'd see blue sky. Sometimes all I saw were shades of grey. We'd be pummelled with torrential rain, violently rocked, and we'd have to tense our bodies to try not to hurt each other. Every hour felt like twenty-four. I became an onion of anxiety, with stinky layers of salty fear wrapped around my panicking heart.

I tried to keep my hands to my ears and wished the thundering engine would stop.

Until it did.

Then I cursed my wish. What'd I'd meant was for the *sound* to go away, not the very means by which we achieved forward motion through an angry sea.

The waves sounded more threatening without the engine. As we drifted and bobbed and swayed, I became obsessed with stretching my neck to peer over the heads of those between me and the porthole. I hoped to see land on the horizon. I hoped I would not see pirates.

Soon it was clear we were being towed. By 4518. The two boats never lost sight of each other, and like good sisters, they had learned to share. When towing us became too much for 4518, her engine would stall. Passengers on our boat would jury rig a fix, and our engine would sputter back to life. For a time. When we stood still on the ocean—the engine having failed, again, we'd get hooked up to the overfilled sister boat, which tried her best to help advance our position while more solutions were found and parts invented.

I imagined that we were two wooden specks on a blue and green planet. We may have looked seaworthy from Karma's great height, but up close, it was horrific—the holes, the rotting wood, the vomit, the sewage.

I wanted to cry: So many beautiful human beings had become a toxic cargo.

Day in and day out, the boats continued a relentless pattern of drifting and motoring in what I hoped was southbound-ness. And I hoped that S meant land.

Sometimes I'd maneuver my way between a mix of slumped and collapsed bodies to get up to the deck for fresher air.

"We are sinking."

The news spread fast. We had to reduce our weight on the water. Many of us tossed our few possessions overboard—a small statue in a bag, a backpack of photos, a wad of passports—to lighten the load.

The result seemed to satisfy the boat. I like to think 4581 let out a sigh of relief. In my dizzied state, I pictured the boat wanting to help us and pushing her thoughts back in history to the trees that her boards once were, to summon some strength of the forest she was born into, then tensing her wooden muscles, and pretending to the point of believing that the new paint would hold her together like a protective covering.

In my dreams, I saw her signalling to her sister, 4518, that there was still a great distance ahead; I heard her whispering her fears at night, or after her twin had fallen asleep and then startled, soothing her nightmares.

Chapter 12

Lost Within Lost

THERE WAS CHEERING, AND MORE cheering. Joy spread along the rows of our bodies.

"Can you see it?" said my father.

"Malaysia!" shouted the captain.

The land on the horizon energized us all. It was still light when we were close enough to see people on the land.

"We could swim from here if we had to," said someone who'd been patching a hole.

An umbrella of relief opened. Shortly we'd be able to feel land under our feet. Maybe there would be some food, a crust of bread or a piece of fruit: My stomach was empty, and my throat was rusty from the salt air. Maybe we could wash. Maybe I could go to the bathroom. It was a lot of maybes, but the sight of land allowed for a million maybes in my mind.

Many of us had clambered up on deck to watch our approach to land. Was this Freedom? And then, terror. Shock. My knees became jiggly. Uniformed men were pointing guns. At us. At me.

They gestured to the captains of our broken boats to turn around and head back out to sea. Several hopped into their own boats, approached us, and shouted orders to turn around.

When 4581 and 4518 didn't move fast enough, they hooked ropes to our fragile sides and dragged us back out to the rough ocean.

"Perish at sea for all we care," I imagined them saying.

We were stunned. Women wept, children sobbed, and babies wailed because their mommies were crying. Men reacted to defeat with anger, silence, tight lips, gestures— many trying to choke back their tears. More people collapsed, their bodies contorted in spasms of sickness. Some died. Images of a new life in Freedom faded, as did spirit.

By nightfall, the boats bobbed in the open water. We were unwanted. Just more drops in the ocean. In my mind, I travelled back to before my grandfather left, to the workroom and the words of workers in our business and neighbours. *"Millions of people are fleeing. Some on land and others by sea. There are pirates out there. Resisters are tortured in jails. Refugee camps are no better—a death sentence."*

I tried to count our days and nights. I got to seven but began doubting my greatest strength: my math. The morning after having guns pointed at us, when we were out in the rough sea, I saw a ship. Others did too. Hopes rose again. But the captain ordered us all to stay below decks, telling us that the vessel was Russian.

"Communists," I heard, and something about us all being dead soon.

But whether they saw us or not, the Russians didn't bother with us.

We drifted some more. And then it happened: A massive slab of grey that was not the ocean came upon us. Right beside us. I thought we would be swallowed. A giant cargo ship, towering over our tiny vessels. We were invited aboard, but we'd have to climb the tallest ladder I had ever seen. We were all weak. I used every ounce of my strength to climb up, up, up, and up the side of the ship. I lost track of how many rungs as my shaking hands, legs, and feet precariously clung to and climbed the ladder while carrying one of my younger siblings across my chest.

The captains and a few people to help keep the engines running remained on 4518 and 4581. They were looking up at us, small like ducks in the water waiting for scraps of bread.

Someone produced a large red tin of soda crackers and colas with red labels. I imagined the soda crackers coming out of an oven, puffy and warm. I licked the salt off the top, then oh! next came the crunch between my teeth, the satisfaction of crumbs on my tongue, the layer of not-too-wet cracker along the roof of my mouth, the exquisite pleasure of having food in my mouth and my belly eager for me to swallow. I sipped a fizzy explosion of bubbles from the cola, the sweet liquid pooling on my molars, awakening my gums.

Somehow it reminded me of pho. In that lifesaving moment, I could have inhaled cracker crumbs forever and been eternally happy.

I fell asleep on the great grey creature in the sea. I dreamed of riding a giant sea turtle toward a happy ending that included another sighting of land, this time without the guns.

CHAPTER 13

LETUNG, JEMAJA

NOT EVERYONE WHO HAD BOARDED 4581 and 4518 had survived, and not everyone on the broken boats were on the giant ship-turtle, but the difference in numbers didn't account for how much more space there was for us. I'd stretched my whole body out, barely touching my siblings while I slept. The grey-painted metal floors felt softer than the best mattress at home.

I opened my eyes and pulled myself to a sitting position, then stood stronger than I had in days. My feet were solid on the deck, the waves below no match for the size and weight of this ship. It was hard to imagine there was an ocean below.

"Om mani padme hum." It was a whisper, the Buddhist equivalent of hallelujah.

"Grandfather?" I turned in a circle. But he was not there.

"We are going to be processed," my father said.

"Processed?" I could not conceive of a reason we needed "processing." We needed land, food, and a bathroom.

"Our names are on a list, Vi Tu," said my father. "Where we are going, people will count us and check our names off that list and take care of what's next."

Order, process, numbers. Accounting and digits. This was the language I knew best. Hope had arrived, and it had a plan.

Getting on and off the boats and the ship took time and zapped energy, like everything we did as a group. But the promise from Hope about Freedom helped me endure.

Just behind the beach was a huge clearing. It was still sand, but there were mats on the ground in roped-off sections. Smaller groups of people who had been ahead of us in the line now occupied the mats in several of the sections. After the crowded conditions on the twin sister broken boats, the space between the people, even more space between the groups, and the land beneath them were marvels.

When my feet touched the firm ground, I said a silent "Thank you" and fell into a line with my family where we shuffled toward our assigned roped-off section of mats. A man arrived with a large clipboard and a thick pad of paper, and with the help of a translator, he explained that we were in Letung, on the island of Jemaja. My heart fell when he said we wouldn't be staying; this was a registration place only.

We were fed several meals a day. We were given water to drink. There were areas designated as latrines—still primitive, not very private, but better than that single cesspit for all 300 of us on 4581. We were checked and counted and listed and catalogued. I had patience, though, assuming we would soon be heading somewhere away from the beach, farther inland, on this island.

When I had counted fourteen days, I spotted officials heading out to the spot where 4581 and 4518 sat bobbing in the bay, and I began to shake.

I didn't want to be at sea again. But I was pushed into another snaking line and made to board 4518, where we all went to our original spots. From what I could glimpse through the porthole, a powerful-looking vessel was lashing a heavy line to us. It began towing.

Soon we were going faster than ever before. I worried 4518 couldn't withstand the impact of the waves at this speed. Nevertheless, hours passed.

"It's an island," someone called out.

The towing vessel pulled near the shore, then released us into shallows.

There was no one on the beach. No buildings. No clearing or ropes and no areas in which to organize people.

"It's uninhabited!" someone else yelled.

"We're being dumped in the middle of nowhere!" said another. I was sure this wouldn't, couldn't be true, that once we stepped onto the island we would see.

"Swim or wade," another passenger shouted.

"Help your brothers and sisters," my father said to me. Of course.

I resorted to counting the people again, trying to soothe my growing panic. But it didn't work. The boat bounced and pitched as people leapt from different spots around the rails.

"At least it will be safer than the sea," said my mother.

I helped my parents get the youngest children into the water, then I jumped too. It wasn't very deep, but I still went under. When I surfaced, I stared at the landmass and watched the so-far-uninhabited island open her eyes and prepare for an onslaught. I waded ashore wearing the same clothes I'd been wearing since we left our home that I could not call Saigon.

How long were we to be here? Where were the officials to catalogue and organize and feed us? Where were the bathrooms? So many of us—500 or 600 people, including my family of eight, had waded to shore, and were left to create a community. To make something from—and with—nothing. And for how long? There were no bathrooms. Where was the food? My upbringing and duty demanded I be grateful, but now that I was off the boat, even though I'd left my grandfather's black mood back in Vietnam, I had mixed emotions. How could I be grateful for being alive and angry at the same time?

"*Gratitude, Vi Tu,*" whispered my grandfather.

"For what?" I said. "I have nothing."

"*You have everything,*" he told me.

I lay on the sand, a stretched-out starfish, no longer cramped on the boat, and began to cry. Nobody noticed because I was a quiet crier, and they were crying too.

"Why couldn't I come with you to China?" I asked my grandfather. I rolled to my side and focused on the tiny crystals of sand—thousands of amber jewels that I wished would open a magic portal to a real life.

"China is my home," he said.

"But I am your boy."

"You need to grateful," he said.

"No," I said. "I need to be your boy,"

"You have your own soul now, Vi Tu."

"You mean, I was your boy." I covered my eyes with my hands.

A million feelings battled inside me, including a thick layer of terrified. But Grandfather's words had created a shift. I tried to bring anger to the front, but it would not come. I tried to hate. And then a little crab poked through the sand, and softness entered my heart.

"I miss you, Grandfather," I said silently through my tears.

There was earth under my feet. My name had been written down on a form.

My parents were not in jail. Me and my brothers and sisters were alive, and we were not begging on the streets. *Where there is food,* but I turned away from that thought. We'd not been assaulted by pirates. I would not drown. My bed was an island.

It had to be enough. Because it was all there was.

"Now, thank forward, Vi Tu," said my grandfather.

I turned over to my other side. No one was there. I went flat to my back again because I could—because there wasn't vomit, or a dead body, or a dying child, or rotting boards.

I couldn't tell if the current that flowed over me was the ocean or the breeze, it was so gentle. I had this moment. That was the present. I had the next moment. That was the future.

I thanked the future, ahead of when I would arrive in it, in a kind of trust that helped me be calm about what might happen next. I said "Thank you" to the river I hoped would be on this island, for we would need fresh water. I said "Thank you" to the bathrooms we would build on this island. I just kept trusting-thanking-breathing.

"Thank you," I whispered to the ice truck, the temple, and the people who had built the temple.

"Thank you," I said to the cargo ship, to the people on the cargo ship, to the people who had built the cargo ship.

"Thank you," I said to 4581 and 4518, for getting us to this island. I looked up then, out to the old broken boats. They seemed to be collapsing in on themselves, tilting, their skeletons, more patches than planks, dissolving beneath the surface into the hungry mouth of the ocean—the Pacific Ocean, the South China and Java Seas competing for each crumb.

Soon they were gone.

Chapter 14

The Island

THERE WERE NO GRAVES ON the first day, mainly because there were no shovels.

While we were on Letung, I overheard that of all the people fleeing Vietnam by boat, more were dying than were making it to these islands. The abacus in my brain rapidly told me not to think about how many had died. The first night, I thought how from above we must have resembled puddles of creatures huddled together. Each travelling group, whether family or simply a collection of solo journeyers, spread out along the beach at the foot of the treed mountain, disappearing into sleep.

When the sunrise woke the island, we woke too—we were part of her, this nature. "Now you can find the earth's clock and create your own way to mark time," the island said to me when I opened my eyes. In that moment, it was like it was no longer the Year of the Dragon, no more months, no more centuries. I was ageless.

But we still had roles, and mine continued to include caring for the youngest in our family while my parents joined a group of doers and thinkers. It looked like they were in a classroom, except it was outdoors and there were no rows or desks. Some pointed and gestured, others made drawings with a long stick on the damp sand, like schoolteachers. They reminded me of my grandfather when we were in the compound or at the market.

I imagined they were planning like the island was a big company, with lots of departments where people worked. Like our family business, only bigger. This business was called Life. And people in this island Life business would need to make anythings from nothings so that everyone could have somethings. Or at least the basics.

I knew I'd be doing more than childminding. I wanted to. I'd been through something big—we all had. That big thing was still going on. We were no longer afraid of drowning, but we had to survive.

As the meeting was adjourned, some people began collecting anything useful that had made its way to shore from 4581 and 4518. I worked for my parents. My duties included collecting water and wood. Exactly what my father's and mother's duties were, I wasn't quite sure. There was no time for us to chat about our jobs—sorting out food, fire, and a sleeping area for our new life on the beach was a full-time and exhausting job. The island may have been filled with lifesaving treasure, but it fought against my attempts to obtain her gems. It took forever to collect enough water for our family of eight; wood was far away and took ages to cut with the tiny knife I was given for the job.

But I was a good listener while I worked. I learned that one of the departments handled exploration, and another was responsible for organizing hygiene. Because we needed to collect water from the river, we were to wash clothes downstream from the water collection place. No one was to use the river as a toilet—the ocean was the only place for that. It was a step up from the bathroom on the boat, but we still defecated side-by-side, in full view of everyone else.

There was so much do be done, yet many people moved slowly. But they smiled at each other and chatted freely in a kind of pleased-to-be-active way.

More boats arrived and let off more people—sometimes just a few, other times many. They blended with our original group. The teacher-adults gave a lot of directions and set up a designated meeting place so that the new people would learn how things were organized. One day longer on the island than the next person meant you could be responsible for showing them the route to a coconut grove or the path to the place where it was best to collect water from the river. Each of us had skills that were valued, and we were encouraged to share them. When someone found a more effective way to open coconuts than had been known the day before, word spread. If someone discovered a kind of wood that burned hotter, longer, and better, that news was quickly passed along. When I had found a way to polish coconut shells with rocks to make smooth dishes, I shared, and others began to do it. Each discovery or invention took us a little further past survival. We were still wild, but we weren't as dirty as when we'd been on the boats; we didn't have private bathrooms, but at least it didn't smell. We had seen each other at our strongest and at our weakest, sometimes at the same time. Cooperation was critical. I could feel the bond. If this experience had been a story in a book and my teacher had asked me to write a report about it, I would have written across the top of the page:

COOPERATION. INNOVATION. INSTINCT. SURVIVAL. DEAL WITH THE DEAD.

Dealing with the dead was one of the big departments, and nearly every one of the men was required to take a turn doing the work of grave digging. Some people did not live another day.

"Children should not have to face their own mortality," one of the more studious adults said. I had to ask my mother what that meant.

One day, I saw a man who sat with his back against a tree. He had the same dark cloud over his head that my grandfather had before he left for China. The next day, the rain from that dark cloud had washed away the man who had been there. I didn't count the deaths, or the births, I just looked away a thousand times, avoided the graveyard beyond the growing boundary of our encampment, and tried not to mix up the darkness of night with the darkness of spirit.

"Good night," I said to my family.

"Good night," I said to my mother.

Chapter 15

Buddha in a Boy

I LAY ON THE SAND under the black velvet blanket of the universe, a sandal-wearing little boy in a pair of shorts and a T-shirt, every stitch and seam from the threads of his grandparents. As I gazed at the stars, I wished for a little bit more than just enough. For me. For all of us on this island.

The steady hum of sewing machines accompanied my dream. I looked for my grandfather but found myself standing instead by my father's side, waves lapping against our ankles. He stared straight ahead, silent, and I saw he was a man with a massive burden. My dream morphed into something black and ominous, my heart thudding so hard it pressed on my lungs until I couldn't breathe. The night terror woke me, and I reached for my grandfather with my mind and my soul, but he would not come. I saw myself as a preschooler who once knew his way to one of the largest marketplaces in the world, who always seemed to have the responsibilities suited to someone much older. I wished for a magic time machine that would take me to my future in Freedom and then bring me back to this beach on this island, where I would lie under that same night sky, see the same stars, think the same thoughts, except then I would know it would all turn out okay.

My chess-mind never stopped thinking—in several languages and dialects. Was it karma that kept me and my family—and so many others—alive for another day? Was it the voices of a thousand ancestors? Was it that all the world's prayers were sent up to the sky and gathered with a soft tether before descending over our little stretch of beach like a protective bubble? Perhaps it was all of it, wrapped in a blanket of gratitude.

Except it didn't protect me from the flashbacks.

"Silence. That ship might be Russian. Their crew will kill us."

"There are pirates out there."

"There is no life left in our boats. But we will be shot if we proceed to port. We must head back to sea."

During the day, I tried to accept that I lived on a single mountain that rose from the ocean and stretched its beach and forest toward the sky. My feet became used to it all. They had to. It was a long, uphill trek to fetch water. I collected it in coconut shells. Small but able-bodied, I combined my sense of duty with my enjoyment of healthy competition with myself. I made a carrier out of tree boughs to go across my shoulders so that I could hang some water containers on each side, then set a target and worked to beat that target of quantity and time for each trip.

To gather wood for the fire that cooked our fishy soup, which was wet and proved to be poor fuel, I had to hack away at trees for ages, the tiny knife cutting my skin when it slipped against the tree bark. But I tried to distract myself by noticing how different this tropical forest was from my old life in the city and its markets, houses, electric fans, and factories. Chickens, yes, but wild animals and unrecognizable insects and snakes, no. Here, we relied on experience, sometimes tragic, to tell us whether a plant was poisonous. My legs, like those of most of the children, looked as if they'd been hacked by machetes.

It seems like my former life had only been a dream. I'd eaten pho in restaurants. Sold exquisitely tailored shirts my family had manufactured to US soldiers. Attended private school. Won accolades for my calligraphy—then Banh!

Bang! I was in another world: sucking on the bone of a fish that made my skin break out in hives, hauling water down a mountain and then climbing back up to collect more—it might as well have been a hundred times a day that I had to climb that mountain. I climbed it for water, yes, but also to try and block the images of death all around me, each one hitting me like a physical blow.

Each sunrise melted into many. One morning, one of my brothers became delirious with fever and so weak that a darkness came over my mother's face. I held my tears in my throat to be strong for her and for my brother. Miraculously, among us was a medical doctor, and even more miraculously, he'd managed to bring some medicines with him. He offered some for my brother. When my father offered to pay, the doctor refused. We were all in this together, he said. My brother recovered. My parents, brothers, sisters, and I were indebted to the doctor for his generosity.

More than a thousand of us crunched paths and trails going into the jungle in search of wood, water, and coconuts. Our feet made hard-dirt sidewalks to popular spots, including the graveyard. Big boats arrived with basic supplies to supplement the fish and coconuts we could collect and share, or those we purchased. Broken boats filled with exhausted people were towed as close to the island as possible on a regular basis.

I was glad to be a distance from the beach when officials arrived. Hundreds swarmed the boat, some getting crushed or drowned. Shoulder to shoulder, young and old, people would try to get an official's attention to ask a question, or to listen for their name should there be a letter posted from a safe country or from a relative that had miraculously found its way to the island. Others held envelopes high in the air that they wanted carried off the island to aid organizations who would in turn get their letters to loved ones. The return address on these letters was now Air Raya. Apparently, the island had been given a name, or we'd finally been told the one it had.

My drive to survive clapped its powerful hands over my ears and filtered out sounds of suffering. The sun blinded me against the faces of other hungry children, or perhaps it was the ash in the air from fires that boiled the water and cooked the fish that kept us alive clouding my vision. The wind turned my head from our free-for-all, wide-open ocean bathroom and from our crude living conditions. When I wasn't gathering wood or hauling water, my fingers found a rock, and I polished coconut shells to become dishes.

The values of my ancestors, led by masters Lao Tzu and Buddha—respect, sincerity, gentleness, service—were vocal, constantly messaging from my heart to my brain, but it was my muscles that were called to duty. At the end of the day, I would fall to my knees and give thanks for the cooler night temperature, pray for a dreamless sleep, and lie on the mountain that had risen from the sea a million lifetimes ago.

Chapter 16

Leg of Hope

I think the blackflies knew about it before I did. I was hacking at a branch with the little knife, as I did every day, when, somehow, I either stepped or stumbled in a thicket of sharp ends. It was like an animal had bitten into my thigh. But the tooth was really a branch. One end was attached low to a tree. The other end was inside my leg. Blackflies found the wound before I could pull my leg off the sharp sword of the tree. Blood dripped onto the bark. The swarm of blackflies divided itself between my injured leg and the stained bark. I could see the bone.

The blackflies followed me all the way to our beach encampment.

"It would be good to know if that tree is poisonous," my father said, giving me something more to worry about. He covered the wound with some strong paper.

"Is that money?" I asked, recognizing an American dollar bill.

"It's strong, like gauze," he said. "What else will we do with it? It's not like there is anything to buy here," he said, wrapping my leg with a strip of cloth.

Soon my wound was seeping a greenish slime.

"He could lose his leg," I heard my mother whisper. How would I gather wood then?

One day, as I limped about doing the chores I could, a loud cheer rose from our beach community. I looked to the water where a large boat, obviously well-cared for and so different from the dilapidated vessels we were used to seeing, approached shore. There were only a few people on board, and soon they were on shore, spending a little time with those of us who needed medical attention.

When it was my turn, the friendly doctor inspected my wound, cleaned it and applied some sort of salve, and then replaced the goopy American bill with clean dressings. Through an interpreter, he said, "You're going to be just fine—now."

Relief filled my heart. I turned the doctor's words into "You will leave this place." It did not matter that it was not what he said. But I clung to what had just occurred: People knew we were here. They'd come to save me, and there had to be a reason.

I watched the vessel disappear back toward wherever it had come from and swallowed something the doctor had left behind—a seed of inspiration.

Beyond all reason, from our primitive, barely survivable living conditions, I felt that seed begin to sprout.

I *would* be well.

I would serve others.

I would become a doctor.

Every day thereafter, when I walked to the stream to collect water or hiked into the forest to find firewood, I imagined myself as a doctor. With every cry that rang out in the night—which signalled someone in our community of more than 500 had died—I pushed myself into the vision of helping others. I did not know what country this future-me would be in, but I could see myself with a healed leg and a real home, and going to school to become a doctor.

If my grandparents could walk over three million steps from China to Vietnam, build a thriving and successful family clothing and textile business, fund a school, and donate to hospitals, then I could become a doctor.

I wanted my feet to get used to walking the walk of a healer.

Chapter 17

Enterprise

People who lived on nearby islands came in tiny boats, ready to do business with us. They offered to sell us things they'd grown themselves or that they'd stolen from somewhere else. They offered us shopping trips to Letung, the place where we'd been catalogued.

"Maybe we can afford to go to Letung with one of those people with a boat," my mother whispered.

"There is bound to be better food there than this horrid fish," said my father, looking into his coconut-shell dish.

At the thought of wandering around market stalls, I bit down on my lip to stop from missing-home crying. I squeezed my eyes tighter so as not to imagine our market stall at Bến Thành. Then I pretend-tasted the food I imagined *might* be at the market we *might* go to. "How can we pay them?" I asked my father, looking down at my leg where the American bill used to be.

He tugged on the waistband of his shorts. And then he told me. Some families, including our own, had money sewn into the clothing they wore. After all, most of the passengers who had been able to pay in gold for their passage were professionals or highly skilled workers—many of them had also been able to save for their new life in another country. My father had sewn fifty American dollars and a few pieces of jewelry into his clothing. Well, he had forty-nine dollars now: That's where the makeshift bandage for my leg had come from.

"When your uncle went to Australia, he put gold plates in his shoes," he said.

Gold plates inside his shoes? I was fascinated and eager to hear more, but my father was not the storyteller my grandfather was.

With a trip to Letung still hanging in the balance, the next offer from the visitors was to build huts for us. One thing was certain: We were all sick of sleeping outside on the beach. Perhaps it was time for us to benefit from a roof and some walls and some privacy.

The huts were a problem for my chess-mind. While it was true it would be nice to have better shelter from the sun and rain and wind, a hut also suggested permanence. You pay for a home when you are planning to stay. My grandfather built our business and homes on a plot of land, and we stayed put. If our family had a hut, did it mean we'd be here a long time? Forever?

"Some things are too good to be true." My grandfather whispered to me from the top of a coconut tree.

So it was that our family, and many others too, agreed. We paid those business-minded folks their money and in return were disappointed. After harvesting materials from our island and hauling them to our beach, they built not huts, plural, but one hut. A single long, narrow rectangle. A shed. The kind of structure farmers would build to protect harvested crops: one common roof and four outer walls. Inside there were no dividing walls. We were expected to keep ourselves in our own area. We had a roof and a back and front wall, but to each side of us was another family.

We immediately set about finding a way to create some sort of divider to mark our space and obtain some privacy. My father bought some canvas. Some of it we hung as walls to divide our little space; the rest we placed, like a mattress pad, over a rectangle of tree bark—not even a platform—on which we all slept together. Sometimes simplicity brings comfort. Sometimes. The bed was like a bed of nails. The canvas mattress pad did little to stop our scratching from the bark. I preferred when we'd been on the sand.

The hanging walls did little for our privacy and nothing for our security. There were times when my father purchased cigarettes from those other-island visitors. He'd put the package down in our hut-space and later find it had been lifted. My father would be angry then. I'd just wonder why he thought cigarettes were a necessity, with our limited resources and struggles to survive.

The contrast between our world and most of the rest of it was bizarre. Life was a fusion of primitive living with modern times. Most of the time, I was shirtless, which was ironic given the family business had been to manufacture them. Some knew how to fish but had nothing—not even a small amount of money. I cut down trees with a small knife to get wood for the fire, but we had matches. We bathroomed from a platform extended out into the ocean. We ate horrid, stinky fish soup from coconut shells. Someone had a guitar, and another even had a camera with film in it. Fusion.

The camera reminded me that, outside our world on this island, new products were being debuted at the stalls at Bến Thành. All over the world, American movies were playing in theatres, and classical musicians were performing on stages to huge audiences. Yet here I was, hacking at a tree for hours until I could fell it.

How long would my small knife last? How many fires might we have before we had no tool to cut down the trees? Would we be here so long that we will have cut down all the trees? I asked myself these questions.

My father began to engage in more mature conversations with me, including about money. He told me that a delivery had come through the Red Cross, and a hundred American dollars had reached us from my grandfather in China. The cataloguing system had worked: Mail—with money in it—had reached us. My father said he'd decided we could afford to go to Letung.

I would go with my mother and father, and we would buy things that had been donated by other countries and had been intended for us but had been stolen and were now available for sale. Even with my grandfather's $100, I knew our waistband money and jewelry would not last forever.

Chapter 18

Shock and a Promise

THE MARKET ATMOSPHERE IN LETUNG was as colourful and bright as the vegetable stands that lined its streets. It seemed so normal, so much like Bến Thành with its vendors, their voices and calls, the smells of fresh vegetables and fruit, and rotting ones too.

I was no longer the small child who became terrified when separated from his grandfather at Bến Thành. I split up from my parents and began to explore. My parents would be purchasing food if they could find something affordable. I was happy to be my own person, away from my family instead of a constant part of them. The temporary independence gave me new energy, and I zipped in and out of the spaces between stalls and then checked out the streets and alleyways of Letung. There was no purpose to my little adventure—I was simply free. Free from hauling water, free from collecting firewood, free from watching my siblings. I was breathing easier, my feet almost dancing.

I turned a corner and saw a slight woman in ragged, dirty-looking clothes, somewhat bent, pawing through the waste behind a market stall. My heart ached for her. I watched the woman, so weak, desperate, sadness flowing from her into the wavy humidity.

Then I recoiled, and my heart broke in two.

The woman was my mother.

I raced down an alleyway and leaned against a pillar. It was not supposed to be this way! I stayed there until I could catch my breath, wiping my face with my arm. The vivid greens and bright yellows of the market faded to black and white as I saw the life she was living—six children and a husband to feed.

I put the pain I felt for her, the shame I felt for being homeless and poor, and the sorrow for our family's fall from respectability into a compartment deep in my soul. I squeezed my eyes shut until I felt determination swirl its energy around hope and rise to my surface. Alone, yet among hundreds of vendors and buyers and stalls, a flame flickered and set fire to responsibility and, fueled by it, ignited my sense of duty and became a raging, solemn promise: When we were no longer refugees, I would shift us from the poverty that had befallen us. I would not allow my mother to feel the need to rummage through rubbish bins for food again. I was the golden child. I could not let this happen to my mother. She would always be provided for.

My grandfather had led me through the market in Saigon many times, then my father had brought me to this one in Letung. Both men had been decision makers in their family's finances. I vowed to make my own decisions, good ones that considered their advice but were wholly independent and that would benefit those I loved.

We returned to our island and family and hut-space, where I learned that my father had made a baffling financial decision at the market: He had purchased a large amount of candy, thinking himself a new kind of refugee-preneur perhaps, and spread out the sweet goods for sale.

What was he thinking? No one had any mad money—not the kind of money to buy nonessential sweets from yet another middleman, especially when those things weren't essential. But my father insisted there were people on this island who had much more money tucked away than we did, and he had hoped they would buy our sweets. I thought of my father's cigarettes and thought perhaps he was right.

It was a stab in the dark, a launch of a faulty firework, a throwback to who we had been: vendors in a free market system. Nobody bought our sweets, but it did bring sugar-induced silly smiles to our sun-scorched faces as we consumed the whole inventory.

We made many more trips to the market of Letung, despite the risks of the boat trips and the ever-declining funds. I started to wonder why we'd always return. Why didn't we bring the whole family to the market, escape, and attempt to fade into the population of Jemaja? There was no guard on those trips or on the island where we lived. Then I realized that doing that would forever remove the chance of us being moved to a real country if we were missing from the roll call that might someday occur, if the cataloguing months before meant more than Red Cross mail delivery. Our only hope was to stay put, in the place where someone, somewhere, had our names on a list.

Chapter 19

Air Raya to Galang

"Banh! Banh family of eight!"

This time, the officials were looking for us. For us! It was magical.

"You will come with us now," they said. "We will take you to Galang."

Suddenly, we were not in the crush of bodies that surrounded the boat; we were *on* the boat. The boat was seaworthy, and there were fewer people on it than when we'd arrived on Air Raya. Though I still had no possessions, I knew my family and I were closer to being in a forever home in that place I less frequently thought of as Freedom.

Pulau Galang was laid out as a system of buildings and paths that went inland for quite a long way. There were bridges, arches, buildings like a small temple or church, and some offices. Construction workers were just finishing the longhouses there—but they were different than the huts that had been built on Air Raya. Plus, we didn't have to pay for them. Four families would live in one combined accommodation area upstairs, with a shared kitchen downstairs. There was an outdoor bathroom—again, to be shared by the four families, and running water from a tap attached to the side of the four-family building.

Privacy was still an issue. But I did not have to sleep on the ground or on a scratchy piece of bark. I did not have to pee and poop in the ocean. I did not have to hike up a mountain to fill a container with water. Neither did I have to go into the jungle and cut down a tree with a knife.

After a couple of days, I began to feel something I had never felt—boredom. While grateful for the improvements, and thrilled that our change of residency to this new island meant we'd someday be accepted in another country, I had nothing to do. Survival had been a full-time physical job with challenges that did more than prevent me from being bored: It made me more creative in finding solutions.

Waiting was a whole other thing. Time passed slowly. I imagined that over time, the waiting would develop into a black cloud over all our heads. I didn't want that to happen to me. I worked on keeping my chess-mind active by going over lessons from Lao Tzu, studying nature, and calculating with an imaginary abacus.

Everyone on Galang seemed to have a sponsor and a country to go to. Everyone except us. I kept reminding myself that we could be back on Air Raya. Week after week, I told myself being in Galang was one step closer to a country of our own.

One morning, an official and an interpreter visited us. We were interviewed for permission to enter Australia. I became excited because my father's brother was there—the one who had lined his shoes with gold.

My father relied on me to help the translator—there was a lot of asking and answering the same question in a kind of language round. At the end of the interview, my heart began to beat fast. It would be so good to be given a new life.

For whatever reason, the official delivered heart-crushing news. I knew we'd been declined before the interpreter got to translate the answer. My father had been hopeful to reunite with family. It was not to be. Faced with more waiting, and without the distraction of survival, I went inside myself with a combination of gratitude for being alive and a sadness for what we'd once had and now didn't have. Then I'd feel ashamed and guilty for feeling those feelings. We were alive. We had survived at sea when so many had not. Why couldn't I be grateful enough? Why did I feel ashamed of who we were—or who we had become?

I went back to my strategy of knowing we were on Galang for a reason. I pushed myself to be patient.

The sun came out for another day of tropical heat. We were asked to attend an appointment in the office area of the island. "There is a group of people in Canada who want to sponsor a large family," said the translator after the official had spoken to him.

My heart skipped a beat. We were a large family. Six children and two parents.

From that moment on, our lives changed. Hope gave way to dreams almost realized. We were revitalized while in wait mode. Yes, there was always that what-if-they-change-their-minds worry, but I pushed it away. We were going to a place called Canada. I was going to live in Canada.

"Cah-nah-dah." I sounded it out, attempting to make the syllables familiar to my mouth and the mechanics in me that made speech.

"Singapore," the official said. "You will fly to Canada from Singapore."

Soon. One day. At some point.

"Please don't change your mind," I prayed each night. I had nothing to do, I had no possessions, but so long as our sponsors didn't change their minds, I would soon have a country.

Chapter 20

Singapore

I FACED THE WIND AND watched the front of the boat divide the water, trying to pinpoint why this boat felt so different from the others. Then it hit me: it was seaworthy.

Earlier that year, I'd pointed to the S on a compass held by a reluctant captain who didn't know where we were going. I now put my whole heart into the N for North America. I wished I had access to knowing more about its size and people and the way they did things. I wondered if the people were all the same size as the soldiers who bought shirts from me.

"Maybe we'll see some people wearing shirts we've made," I said. But my father was lost in his own thoughts, and my mother was busy with the younger children. I continued with all kinds of imaginings about the people's wealth, freedom, and about becoming a doctor. I created my own scene of tall men wearing tropical print short-sleeved shirts. And then guilt came over me

again. We had escaped from the land of the oppressed and impris-
oned. We'd laboured hard and long among many others who
were doing the same. I wanted sponsorship for everyone and tried
not to feel guilt for our being chosen over the families I knew
were still on Air Raya.

My heart sought a connection with the masters, ached
to understand, needed to walk with Buddha and Lao Tzu
along a road on which I would guide my soul to nature and
nurture.

I put my face to the wind one more time, and the tropical spray carried my grandfather's message. *"Onward in
peace, boy."*

When we spotted land, my father and I went to the back
of the boat. The engine churned up our past—the wake a
timeline stretching all the way back to Vietnam and before.
The pages of our family's story were written on the white of
the wake and the tips of the breaking waves. The pages burst
into the air, then drifted down to the water, where they
floated as white paper boats until they slipped under the
surface. I pictured myself frantically snatching as many chap-
ters as I could, stuffing them into my shirt. I felt the first
stirrings of a need to preserve our story, to be the keeper of
our tale. I stretched out my hand but grasped only misty air.
Wishing did not bring the pages close enough to pluck from
the air or scoop from the sea. I made my heart memorize
everything. *One day, I will write all of this.* I sent my silent
promise to my father as I looked up at him, then out to the
water.

As though sensing my commitment, my father recited an old proverb:

"If we have a little rice, we eat rice.
All we need is a few grains of rice to make soup.
If we have a little, we ration and appreciate what we have.
If we have more, we share it."

Chapter 21

Sky

THE BOAT DROPPED US OFF so close to the Singapore airport—surrounded by water on three sides—that we could have walked to board our flight, except we were several days early, which meant more sleeping on the street nearby. We were still dressed poorly, and we were hungry, and yet, lying there with other refugees, I began to imagine what my new life in Canada would look like.

Then a terrible thought came to me. Maybe the sponsoring just meant we would be allowed to be in Canada, but we would have to sleep on the street there too. I had to ponder that for a while.

After a few days and nights, I found myself in another lineup, only this time it wasn't to board a boat. It was a mammoth-sized plane with a giant red leaf painted on its side and a wingspan so enormous it sucked the air out of my lungs. It did not seem possible that something this big and heavy could get off the ground and stay in the air—let alone for thousands of kilometres across an entire ocean.

I climbed the stairs and into the tubed body of the plane. A friendly smile led me to a seat—my own seat! It was like heaven, softness that absorbed my bony bottom, firm construction that supported my back. And it was like magic too. From the seat in front of me, a fold-down tray materialized. A tray just for me! There was a button on the armrest that allowed my seat to tip back if I put enough weight and pressure on the chair's back.

I smiled at my father. He half smiled back, as if in a trance. I watched my mother's body relax into her seat, each of my brothers and sisters delighted in their own spaces: the tables, paper folders, and seat-tipping-back features.

We all were asked to put on our seat belts. I watched the helpers who looked after us on the plane explain in charades how to put on a mask if it became hard to breathe, or how to put on a life jacket if we crashed into the ocean. *If we crashed into the ocean?* We'd just been on the ocean. *Might we go there again?* The helpers smiled a lot, so I decided it was not a big risk.

Then the plane's engines roared, some of the children cried, and a woman seated across the aisle gasped. My comfortable chair pulled me into its cushioned back as the plane thrust forward. It sped down the runway until I felt the wheels leave the ground. I looked out the window and thought we might dip right into the sea, but the ocean receded until the boats looked like toys. Higher still we rose, thousands of islands poking up from the sea that we had bobbed about on and lost count of our days. I followed the lines of the land and sea below, their blue and green mottled patterns like the globes I'd seen in school, then the clouds covered my window.

Plates, chopsticks, food, and hot tea in silver pots arrived on a wheeled cart that travelled up and down the centre aisle of the plane. It was like a kaleidoscope for my senses: the smell of ginger and new plastic, tinkling utensils and murmuring voices, the drone of the engines, the whiteness of the light through the windows, and the taste of freedom at the back of my throat. How long could I make space for it all?

I should have known about magic seats and giant wings and other worldly things. We'd had a business in a market with thousands of other vendors; I'd been to private school; my grandfather had hired an entire restaurant for a party for me; we'd been wealthy. But the simplicity of my life so far weighed heavily upon me. I was a little boy who liked pho, sold T-shirts in a market, played chess, won calligraphy prizes, and did math on an abacus. And then we'd been homeless. Correction: We were still homeless. None of it prepared me for what I saw on the plane.

I could sleep in this chair. I could live in this seat with this little table.

My Vietnamese-ness became a line of dominoes, which the takeoff tipped and set about a chain reaction of all the things I did not know. Every moment, I was discovering more things I did not know. It was too much, too fast. I had to keep closing my eyes to shut out the fear that, at any time, someone could place an imaginary gun against my temple, pull its trigger, and shout Banh! Bang! and take all this away. Was it okay to be excited? Could I be excited and responsible at the same time? Could I fulfill my duty to serve my parents and still enjoy all the new things that would be outside of the airplane? Would I be able to do all that and become a doctor and make it so that my mother would never have to go through the rubbish at the back of a market? Remembering Letung's back alleys took away my pleasure for the moment. I chased it away by feeling the comfort of the chair. Did Canada have markets? I hoped that if they did, they were not filled with the products that were from that black one where the items had been stolen by bad people from good people to be given to poor people. I told myself that would not happen in my new country, and that there would be lots of rivers in Canada where traders had been selling their wares since the beginning of time.

I burdened myself, my mind going to all kinds of dark corners and through uncharted territory. I tied a thousand knots in my mind and belly to work through why I was here. Who was I? Who would I become? How could I allow myself excitement when I knew survival came before that emotion? Plus, I'd promised to tell our story. What would that look like? I was a math kid with a chess-mind. I didn't know about storytelling.

Thank goodness the drone of the engines put me to sleep. I hid in my dreams as best I could, leaving my fears to dig a little tunnel and burrow near my heart, allowing the story-promise to my father to file itself away on the shelf of an old bookcase in my mind. While I slept, I dreamed that beside the seed of becoming a doctor sprouted a weed. A boat weed from the filth on 4581. It was a stubborn weed and snaked away from the seed of inspiration and headed for my bladder.

When I awoke, we were still in the clouds. It was mind-boggling to me that, almost a year before, we'd been below on the ocean. On the ocean, we feared drowning. We couldn't drown up here. But we could fall. Yet this wasn't a broken plane. The boats were broken. We wouldn't fall. We couldn't. We were going to Canada.

I swayed between questions and statements.

The boat. Was fear of pirates the same or worse than experiencing them? Was fear of drowning the same or worse than swallowing water, having it fill the lungs, then bloating and floating and washing up onshore? Was I afraid of flying? Should I be?

How many tiny boats down there held families like my own? Why was the world like this?

On the plane, there were eight of us. We were free. We were on our way to Canada.

Who were these people we would eventually meet? What would happen first? When would we arrive in this place called Canada?

"Calm, now. There will be time for all these questions later," said my grandfather. "You are in the sky. Feel being a bird."

CHAPTER 22

THE BLUE TOQUE

"Prepare for landing in Edmonton, Alberta," said the captain of the plane. I looked out the window to discover that the colour of the earth on this side of the world was white. All I saw as the plane got closer to the ground were square fields of white.

"That's snow," someone said. "It's January, which is winter here."

My feet vibrated, and my father explained it was the wheels of the plane coming out of the compartment where they'd been tucked away for the whole flight. *Bumpety-bump-bump*, and we were on the ground.

We were getting very good at forming lines, and we created another to get off the plane. As I inched along in it and approached the open door, I began to shiver, suddenly back inside the ice truck. Only this was colder.

And then I was lost in a cloud of fog. Every few seconds, it cleared a bit and then became thicker again. I held my breath: no cloud. I exhaled: cloud. As we exited the plane, so many of us breathing in and breathing out, we created a smoky haze. *Would it always be like this?* When people in Canada were outside, was it hard for them to see each other because of all the breathing clouds? Clouds that stayed visible, crystals light enough to drift away—some floating up to join the clouds, others turning into diamond sparkles on the snow.

When I stopped wondering about the mist, I realized my clothes had hardened. I touched my shorts, and my fingers became wet. I held the hem and thought it might break off.

"You must be freezing," said someone in the welcoming committee.

I pictured my arm or leg stiffening and breaking off, like I thought my shorts might. I panicked and wondered how much longer before I was completely frozen. We had survived tropical conditions with extreme humidity in crowded conditions; now we were in a winter setting, with winds so cold I was sure they could slice me in half.

We were led through double sets of double doors into a large building, where a blanket of warm, safe air surrounded me. I started to defrost immediately. Next, we entered an area where we were sprayed with disinfectant from a large hose and given clean clothes to wear. We moved through this process with as much dignity as we could, accepting the procedure as necessary for a free life.

"We do not want to be sent back," said one of the refu-gees near me and my family. "We're not in any position to complain."

I dared not complain. Even about winter. Even when my tropical body resisted going outside and my skin reacted to the dry air and freezing temperatures. I chose to focus on the wonder that humans could live in such extremes, and marvel at the white stuff that came from the sky.

"You'll only be here for a few days," said an official in the giant processing hall. "Toronto is your destination."

I had only just started to practice saying Ehd-mohn-tohn. Now I would try a new place: Tohr-hon-toh. I practiced inside my head while I was given a new set of clothes, including a winter coat, mittens, scarves, boots, and the most amazing hat that had the palest, most beautiful blue-colour pompom on the top. The pompom that made me a couple of inches taller, warmed my head, and kept the wind from nipping my ears. I fell in love with that hat the moment it snugged and sized itself to me.

I slept in dormitory rooms where soldiers-in-training had slept. I ate huge meals served by smiling Canadians who asked me how I was doing in obviously recently rehearsed and poorly pronounced Vietnamese. Each asker's face would loosen in a half-smile that told me they were hopeful they had said it right and terrified I might speak back in the same language, inviting engagement when they knew only the one Vietnamese phrase. It was so kind.

I learned the word soh-ree. People said it if they walked by a little close, or stepped somewhere I was about to, or if a little food spilled over the side of my plate, or if they saw me shiver from the cold. It was a popular Canadian word that I did not know the meaning of at first. There were many interpreters at our disposal, but I was too polite and too fresh-on-the-ground to ask too many questions.

Days later, when our medicals and paperwork were complete, we boarded another flight from Edmonton, Alberta, to Toronto, Ontario, and Pearson International Airport. I tried not to worry about learning another language and blocked out the what-nexts swirling in my mind. Instead, I grinned when yet more food arrived for that amazing little fold-down table and thought about the magic of people and paper and the little blue toque that made me so much taller and turned me into a Canadian.

At Pearson International Airport, we followed a Vietnamese-speaking person past security (where no one seemed to smile), went through some opaque glass doors, and saw hundreds of people—smiling at us.

Some of those people surrounded my family. They stretched out their arms to my parents, then to each of my brothers and sisters, and then to me. They spoke so quickly that no matter whether they spoke English or Vietnamese or Chinese, I just couldn't have kept up.

An interpreter made things simpler. They gave us name tags and introduced us to the people who came to pick us up. The new people tried out our names. Then, through the interpreter, we attempted to answer a thousand questions.

"How was the flight? Are you warm enough? Are you hungry?"

"Welcome to Canada and the province of Ontario."

"Welcome to your new home."

The noise and chatter rose in a crescendo that threatened to drown out the exchange of translations from English to Vietnamese and then back again. But I still picked up a few things.

This airport was the busiest in Canada.

It was named after something called a "former prime minister" whose name was Lester B. Pearson.

Apparently, Mr. Pearson stood up for the Vietnamese and disagreed with the United States's turn away from the South. I tried to file that away, but it was difficult when everything was coming through an interpreter, and I was tired, excited, and scared and didn't know what was happening next.

We were told that while Toronto was the city we'd landed in, we weren't going to be living here. Instead, we'd be taken to a house outside some town called Uxbridge. Another two new words to practice: Uhx-brih-hdge and tao-hn.

One member of the group of people surrounding my family kept going out of the airport and then coming back in.

"Is he the taxi driver?" my father asked the interpreter.

"He is one of your sponsors, Ted," the interpreter said. "And that's Barbara. They've brought two cars to take you to your new home."

While the interpreter went over some details with my parents, I silently tried out my sponsor's names: T-ehd. Bahr-bah-rah.

I knew nothing about the people surrounding us except the names of these two sponsors. Oh, and that they had stepped forward as a group to be our everything, our lifeline, our angels on earth.

We were divided and loaded into the two cars. I kept my blue toque pulled over my ears and felt the pompom bobbing around. Sometimes I tossed my head just to feel it. I wondered if all Canadian children wore hats like this, and whether they wore them inside the house as well.

The streets were so wide. There were no pull carts or motorcycles. The cars were huge. Every few hundred metres, we had to stop at traffic lights. Eventually, it was stop and start every few metres in a big line of traffic. I watched the car in front of me pull into a parking lot; we followed. There was Chinese signage on the side of the building. They had brought us to an Asian supermarket. I kept my toque on in the store, even though the grocery store was warmer than outside.

"Choose anything you want," said Ted to the interpreter, who then said that to our whole family.

"Anything we want? Are you sure?" I asked the interpreter.

"They want you to feel comfortable with the food you'll take to your new home," said the interpreter.

We must have looked like chaos. We were six children grabbing things from shelves, our mother trying to figure out what we needed, and our father attempting to be patriarchal in the presence of other adults who were being so gentle in balancing their direction of him, respecting his position in our family. We chose too much in a sort of wild shopping spree—so many foods, and quite a few familiar items. "Maybe that's enough," said the interpreter, putting an end to the spree.

In the short distances between car and store, then store and car, my body registered the cold. My eyelashes stuck together. My lips dried instantly. Who knew a season could sting, and winter could bite? The windshield was coated with ice when we came out of the store. Ted had a scraper thing for it.

Everything was so big. There was so much space. Everywhere. Inside the car. Outside the car. Inside the buildings.

With two carloads of people and enough Asian food for a thousand, Ted took the lead car to take us to the place called Uxbridge. We did not know how far it was; we had no sense of time. Tired, with our experiences of almost a year stacking one atop the other, I was a willing passenger collapsed into the seats of a station wagon.

I didn't need to read English to know that the sign said Welcome to Uxbridge because our sponsors played charades by smiling, holding their arms open, and pointing at the sign. We drove through a village, but we did not stop in it. The car climbed a steep hill between snowy fields.

At the top of the hill, we pulled to a stop. In the middle of the field where cows—fatter than the ones I'd seen in Vietnam—ate hay dropped on top of the snow, there stood a large house and a massive barn. Was everything in Canada bigger? The weather more severe? The hills steeper?

The car's tires crunched the snow, packing it as we turned and ploughed up the long driveway. A front porch with railings ran across the front. There was a large tree to the side as well as a wood plank table that had a bench attached to each side. The house had lots of openings for windows. And there was glass in them!

The house was so high on the hill that I was sure it could see the whole world—and I thought if I was on its roof, it would help me see the whole world too.

Chapter 23

The House

The house was big enough that there had to have been children there before, but on our arrival it must have had a hard time following all six of us exploring every nook and cranny. It could not have predicted that the next family it housed had so recently been tossed around on the ocean and forced to forage on an island. It could not have known that the family of eight would step over its threshold, unpack strange foods, wonder over its features, and collapse on its sofas with a brand of gratitude never experienced by the house before. I wondered if it knew that I loved it the moment I saw it.

The house was filled with everything from dishes to sheets. Towels were folded in the bathrooms. Clothes were neatly arranged so that we could figure out what would fit each of us. Knives, forks, and spoons were in a drawer near the sink. Pots and pans were in a cupboard and in a drawer under the four-burner stove. Dish soap, shampoo, hand soap, face cloths, toilet paper, tissues, a broom, a dustpan, a mop, a bucket. It was all there.

Over its solid walls that divided the rooms was a strange surface that consisted of large sheets of paper, with repetitive patterns that matched at vertical seams. They were affixed by glue. Patterned paper glued to walls.

From every window in the house was a view unobstructed for miles. So different than the close quarters of our home in Vietnam, and a complete change from the living conditions on the islands.

I walked down the hallway; there was a room for my parents to have to themselves—it had a bed, blankets, and two little doors that, when opened, revealed a little room with railings and hangers for clothes.

Farther down the hall, there were more rooms with narrower beds that were perfect for children. In the last room, there was a bed for me. It had a mattress that was so soft I wanted to live on it. There was a pillow inside a fabric pillowcase on the bed, just looking at it softened the Uxbridge dreams I'd not yet had. A whole set of sheets, then blankets atop, smelled like the springtime I'd read about in storybooks. There was a little suit as soft as the sheets that I realized was clothing for the night—for me.

Between two of the bedrooms was a room with a toilet, a shower, and a bathtub. Not only that, but there were also taps, with two kinds of water: cold and hot. I'd never known such a thing. In Vietnam, there was one tap that ran warm because of the outdoor temperature. On Air Raya, the water was the stream and the salty ocean. Galang had rudimentary plumbing, a hole in the ground, and a shower-like stall, but no hot water.

"Will I ever get used to this luxury?" I asked the house.

The steam from a shower was magical, and it fogged up the mirror so that I could write my name on it, re-creating the humidity I'd always known.

The hot water wasn't only upstairs. The kitchen had it too. Dishes were washed in hot water that wasn't boiled but came right out of the kitchen tap into the sink.

I met my father in the living room. "So much space," I said.

"And Canadian residency," said my mother. Though she said it in Vietnamese, I could tell she was trying hard with the word "Canadian."

I spent some time trying out every chair and seat in the house—at the table, on the sofa, on an armchair. There were so many places to sit instead of on the floor.

My father tried out the television in the living room—we all gathered round. I thought about if we'd had one in Vietnam, when would we have had the time to watch it?

Though the house stood alone in the middle of open land, it dared the arctic north winds to try to penetrate it. When winter forced its way through a few cracks around windows, the house just made its underground heart pump warmer air through its respiratory system. When the snow attacked from above, the house's roof laughed in weather's face as the pink, itchy, fluffy stuff that I could see sticking out from the attic protected all eight of us: *in-suh-lay-shun*.

When the groceries had been unpacked, instructions on how to turn up the heat, work the faucets and the stove delivered, and the last "goodbye-for-now" was waved and acted out, and before more help and schedules and assistance arrived, we were left in the house on the hill. The house with a view of the whole world.

My family were alone. And if I went to another room, I was alone. Alone behind walls and a door. It was the first time I'd been by myself in almost a year—and the first time I had felt some sense of safety.

There were no limits. None of the borders as in the refugee camps.

There was a remoteness to it that offered a kind of freedom and privacy—no officials, no barracks, no administration office, no shared, primitive toilets—yet it was also isolating. It was a long way to town—to Uxbridge. None of us wanted to walk there in the bitter cold. If we had walked there, none of us would know how to communicate with anyone. I didn't have any money. I had no idea if my father had been given any, but I didn't think so. What I wanted to do was to stay in the sanctuary of the house that could see the whole world. I wanted to start to build my world inside it.

I was adept in several Asian languages, part of a family of successful entrepreneurs in the textile business, strong in mathematics, artful in calligraphy, and a decent chess player. I was from the large city of Saigon, which had fallen and become Hồ Chí Minh City, and I was from stock who walked from China to South Vietnam. But as I sat on my bed in a strange pair of blue jeans and a long-sleeved shirt (and socks!), I thought about how little I knew of the workings of the western world. I had so much more to learn than the English language.

I watched my brothers and sisters form their own bond with the house. One of my sisters would often pause in the hallway at the entrance of her bedroom. She told me that there was often a soldier outside her room—a man in a uniform, not a new uniform, and nothing we'd seen in Vietnam. From hundreds of years ago, she said. No need to be afraid, she said. He'd meant no harm. Even the ghosts of Canada welcomed us, perhaps recognizing we were united by war.

The house on the hill that could see the whole world was never anything but kind to us.

My mother appeared to be happy in the kitchen. My father chose an armchair to represent his paternal role in the house. One night at supper, my parents shared that my mother was expecting another child. There would be a sibling in the spring. The seventh child in our family would be born a Canadian.

Still, I worried. I was to be a student in an English-speaking school. We had no family business in which to work. Soon there would be another mouth to feed and no textile and clothing business to pay for our expenses.

We had become residents of Canada, which was a relief. Yet paradoxically we were less independent than when we were in Vietnam, even less in control than on Air Raya.

I worked hard at understanding how my parents might feel. I could see they had assumed their roles as the heads of the house, and yet I could see by their checking in with each other in an is-it-all-right-that-we-turn-up-the-heat way that they were fully aware that they were under the sponsorship of other adults. The house on the hill that had a view of the whole world was a million miles away from their culture. I watched their eyes squint and their heads tilt when their ears adjusted to new words. I knew my own mouth muscles had to force my lips and my tongue into making new shapes.

I like to think that the house felt the pressure we felt of what was expected of us. And, as all old houses do—especially those ones that can see the whole world—it didn't demand anything from us; it accepted us for who we were. It pushed warm air into each room through a little vented metal mouth in the floor. It watched over us as we slept. It even laughed when we discovered something new. I think the house was so real it even called to an unborn sibling that it knew was going to be born. I felt the safety it offered.

The house on the hill got used to seeing us coming and going. Mostly going. It watched us go to school, it watched us return home, trudging down its long driveway. We became accustomed to glass windowpanes, a furnace, separate bedrooms, even paper glued to the walls.

"You are amazing," I said to the house.

CHAPTER 24

THE CANADIAN TRANSITION

WE HADN'T BEEN IN CANADA five minutes—or so it seemed—but our new Canadian family circle wished me happy birthday and arranged a celebration. I was taken aback by the fuss. I didn't understand. The only time my own family celebrated was for the New Year. We'd never celebrated birthdays. We didn't even use the same calendar to refer to our development—we were Year of the Snake, the Monkey, the Rabbit. Our Vietnamese customs were steeped in the ways of the Chinese.

But my new Canadian family was determined to show me a Canadian child's birthday party. In February 1980, I was a child for an afternoon. A real child! It was expected that I just laugh and smile and eat cake and keep balloons up in the air. My former roles—as a working member of a textile business and now refugee who translated for his parents, and who knew he would become a doctor—were suspended. I knew pure childish happiness for a few hours. And though I was unfamiliar with it, I kind of liked it.

When the party was over, balloons and sparkles scattered through the house, I thought about how earlier that day, at my party, I had not done any work. On Air Raya, I'd worked from morning to night. I had to work to survive. In Vietnam, I'd done chores at home, gone to school, then worked in the business, both at the market and in the compound. Other than the occasional chess game, I only knew work. As I lay in my comfortable bed in the house on the hill, I was overcome with guilt and terror that if I didn't start working, I might not survive. My family might not make it. *Maybe we would be sent back to Vietnam.* I tossed and turned, figuring out how to justify my presence and be part of saving my family. The sleepless night had me thinking about my name and the shame in having such a strange first and last name. And then, as I padded down the hall to the bathroom, I realized it hadn't been that long since I'd last gone to the toilet to pee. "Probably the drinks at the party," I told myself. When I got back to my bed, I reached out for my grandfather's wisdom, but he didn't come to the house on the hill that night. I took the fears that I carried every day and put them in a big sack on my back. Then I tied up my bag of burdens with a thick string of unworthiness.

Needing to go to the bathroom or be near one began to make me aware that something was wrong inside me. The future scientist in me worried that every single cell in me knew about this wrongness, and before each one died, it passed the information to a new cell.

If only shame and unworthiness and the inside-messages from trauma that make a person scared could have been like my leg injury. It had healed. If only it had been like when my skin dried and I thought I had a skin disease, but it just turned out to be the new, dry climate. But it wasn't. I got good at telling myself that it was okay, that I was simply someone who needed to pee more often than others.

It did not cause a physical illness in terms of pain, but the wanting to know a bathroom was close by was a problem that made its way around my bladder and spun shame around my urethra. And I knew, just knew, this was not something to speak about here in the land of perfect hygiene.

Partying aside, right from the start, as the eldest son, I was put in a position of a kind of language valet for my father. The muscles in my mouth were more flexible than his—as was my attitude—so, creating the sounds of English came more easily to me as they filtered through my chess-brain. I had to balance school with being available to attend meetings, fill out forms, and translate for him in all sorts of situations. Those times of translation often led to my father becoming impatient with me.

School registration was one of the first things our family had to handle. Sponsors helped us, and I helped my father register me and each one of my siblings who was of school age. My mother, expecting another child soon, remained at home with the youngest children.

Getting ready to leave for school took ages: boots, hat, jacket, mitts, scarf, and pompommed toque. My younger siblings could barely walk when dressed for the outdoors. Then at school it took almost as long to unlayer those winter clothes and put our outdoor shoes on a rack before changing into indoor shoes. Outdoor clothes dripped melting ice onto rubber mats in the school mudroom. A man came around and cleaned them at night and tidied up during the day. Classrooms contained fewer children than my classes had in Vietnam. There might be twenty-five in one classroom. The rooms themselves were warm and decorated with brightly coloured letters and posters about the subjects we were learning about.

I was placed in grade four when we arrived—that's what they decided based on a combination of not knowing English and knowing a lot of math. Everyone else in my class spoke English. Some came up to me and said hi. I said hi back. I was shocked how the other kids talked a lot to one another during class time, sometimes even when the teacher was speaking. For me, it was different. I was head-down-and-study, the English and Chinese dictionary always close at hand.

Even though I was learning English, I thrived in math. It was reading and writing English that was the problem. During the weekly multiple-choice quizzes, I'd simply choose A and B randomly, which usually netted me three out of twenty questions right. I was so overwhelmed with the new language I wondered, *Why bother reading anything?* My lack of self-confidence prevented me from pushing myself, at first, in reading and writing. I was quiet in all subjects that required speaking. So, I focused on science and math, and later, physics.

The best thing was that no one held an imaginary gun to my head while shouting my last name. *Banh!* They were, however, confused about my first. "Veeee Toooo, is that your last name, son?" "Vee-toe. Interesting. Is that one word or two?"

Vi Tu. It was uncommon. It gave others pause and always led to a question: Is that like DJ? An acronym? Or is it like *Star Wars* and you're R2D2? It got a little silly too. I met a priest named Peter, and when he asked my name and I said Vi Tu, he thought I said "Me too." "That's going to be easy for me to remember," he said. "The same name as mine. Let's go, Peter." In a world of Simons and Cathys and Davids and Janices, I just wanted a name that wasn't followed by a bunch of questions. Eventually, I was able to explain by saying "Vi Tu, sounds like the letter V and the number two." But it took a long time for me to have the confidence and the language skills to explain that—longer to escape the shame of an unusual name and even longer still to embrace the uniqueness of it.

My brain struggled to learn an entire new vocabulary with a different lettering system, then attach it all to an entirely unique culture. But apparently, I was making progress.

"You seem more comfortable with the speed and rhythm of the speech of those around you," one of my teachers said. "Your face is more relaxed."

"Even if I don't understand most of the words." It was not a question. We both laughed.

"Humour is one way that I know someone is learning the language. Jokes are the hardest thing to translate," said my teacher. "And you just made one up."

My younger siblings who were in school had happy stories about their classes. I think they were more absorbent sponges than me. But the older models—my parents—were not quite as spongey as us children. One of my biggest challenges was having Asian-speaking parents who seemed unable to attempt any English. My father pulled me out of school every time he had to deal with someone who spoke English, which was pretty much everyone. Even though my teacher told me I was improving, the forced communication in an adult world on behalf of my parents was exhausting. It might have helped me catch the language faster, but oh, how my brain ached a lot of the time in those adult meetings.

The first few months flew by in a flurry of languages and lessons. During those first few months, it became obvious that my mother would soon have a baby. I became stressed that I'd be translating at the hospital too.

I told myself, one thing was for sure: The new child would always know the way of the snowsuit.

It went as I thought. It was April 16, 1980, Ted's birthday. My father asked me to translate—though the nurses and my mother seemed to know what to do on the day a new Banh entered the world.

My parents chose a western name for their Canadian-born son: Michael. He was golden to me from the first moment I saw his little body, so small was he that he would have fit into my pale-blue pompommed toque.

Chapter 25

Uxbridge 2

There's the church,
and here's the steeple,
open the doors,
and there are the people.
—18th-century children's rhyme
accompanied by hand gestures
that symbolize community

For the first time in my life, we wore clothes made by someone else. With our clothes and so much else gifted by benevolent Canadians. I was reborn in Canada through a massive act of kindness. And I knew it. I was living in a state of perpetual gratitude. Everything I did, even though it was incredibly difficult, was padded or lined with an awe of the underlying goodness of people in my new country. The benevolence of our sponsors, and therefore Canada, was a soft place on which to fall, or a shoulder on which to lean when the going got tough. I knew this from the moment of that blue toque with the pompom was squeezed over my head. Things did get tough—but never in the same way it had been on the boat or the island.

Uxbridge embraced and accepted the "new Canadians" from the house on the hill as one of their families. For several months, visitors from various churches and organizations— some of them strangers to each other even though they lived in the same town—brought kind wishes, gifts of food, and other items they thought we might need or find interesting.

As my English improved, I began to learn about how we had been sponsored. A group of people had come together and approached the government with their "we'd like to sponsor one large family" plan. Because the government required some official organization behind the group, they found a church organization willing to back them.

My every day included dozens of people in our lives— such a large group in the forefront and, no doubt, behind the scenes. To our sponsors, everything appeared to be a reason for celebration. A birthday. A Monday afternoon. A Wednesday morning. A car ride. A break in the weather. A trip to one of their cottages at the lake.

I cannot even calculate how much money was spent on us for dental care, optometrists, and other services that were not covered by national health care. And the interesting thing is that it wasn't their churchgoing that demanded they behave this way; they were just genuinely kind, and they represented their community with a natural ability to see the best in everyone and everything.

Uxbridge was a small place when we moved there. Markham—a much larger centre—was thirty minutes away and had more diversity, but we were not there often. Our transportation to anywhere farther than a long walk and, after a time, a bicycle ride, was wholly dependent on others. The only Chinese speakers I remember in that first year were Dr. Nelson Cheung, the dentist, and Mr. and Mrs. Eng, who owned a large house in Uxbridge.

Ted told me that many of the people in our new life who pooled their love to help us were members of various churches—though one single church took on the role of what Ted said was a financial guarantor, based on the government's requirement for a single representative. To me, there was simply a hugely kind community.

"Caring souls came together under a man named Michael McLuhan, a year before you left Vietnam," said Ted.

"To help people they did not know?" I asked.

"If we really look inside ourselves, we know all people," said Ted.

Ted was like that. He talked to me in a way that reached the child in me: "You gotta play soccer, kid." And he also reached the future me: "We've got to get your father to take a look at these documents, Vi Tu."

On Sundays, I'd tag along with Ted and different sponsors to the churches and faith-services that were true for them. I did it out of respect, and to learn. I kept my own views too. As a Buddhist, I knew Taoism and the values of Lao Tzu, that we are all one family on this Earth.

Ted and Barbara Murphy knew so many people in Uxbridge, and a lot of people knew them. Ted's office had "Chartered Accountant" written on the window. Ted helped me and my father understand the financial aspects of our roles as refugees—from helping us understand the Canadian currency to deciphering a utility bill, and later, how to repay the cost of our flights (which we did). Budgeting and money were things I easily understood.

Together, Ted and Barbara had eight children. Despite her busy household, Barbara was always volunteering. Her work helped build the library and refurbish a church connected to Lucy Maud Montgomery, the author famous for *Anne of Green Gables* who had spent time in Uxbridge during her writing career.

Mary and Lloyd Ball, both teachers, had nine children. Mary called him "Lloyd-ey." Lloyd was a geography teacher, a sweet man who said very little. But when he spoke, his words were pure wisdom. He was patient, clever, and loved fishing. Mary was a substitute teacher who taught French. The Murphys and the Balls were central to my day-to-day and to that of our family. They helped with groceries and encouraged us to have a social life. And then there was Doris Muckle. She had not been at the airport when we arrived, but her presence in our lives, in my life, was like sunshine. Doris had been a nurse in Toronto. Her parents lived in Uxbridge. When they became ill, she left her job in Toronto and moved in with her parents to take care of them. Then she found a position at the post office in Uxbridge. Her input in our lives changed the course of, well, everything. She drove me and some of my siblings to our paper routes, and she accepted us into her home as if we were her grandchildren.

Not long after we met Doris, my father told us the story of how, before we left Vietnam, an oracle had told him he would meet a nice lady who would be our angel. After our family was introduced to Doris, he believed her to be that angel.

Doris had a strong work ethic and you-can-do-it attitude. Some people thought she was too strict, but when she saw in others a willingness to work, she was right in there, supporting and so kind.

The home of Mr. and Mrs. Fowles was my first exposure to Canadian wealth. He was British, she was Jamaican, and they had four children. Back when my father was making three dollars an hour, they would often invite us to their house, and they never looked down on him no matter his job or his wage. They were genuine, caring individuals.

I could see and feel the joy our sponsors experienced from their own giving. I wanted to be on that end of the giving as well—and promised myself that one day I would.

My parents did not want us to be dependent on others, nor did they want us to be rude and reject what was offered to us—we had to learn to graciously accept what others wanted to give and balance that with our own independence. We were not without our own resourcefulness. The walk to town was about half an hour. As the snow melted and spring arrived, we'd walk to town and collect bottles along the way, then trade them for the deposit money so that we could buy groceries.

We had not been in Canada long before Ted helped arrange a job for my father. One of his clients owned a nursing home and agreed to have Dad do custodial work there. I'd watch my father, who was forty years old and extremely thin, riding a twelve-speed bike with skinny tires down the hill to town, and I'd see him coming back up the hill at the end of an exhausting shift. I shivered for him because no matter how bundled he was, he had to have been chilled to the bone.

My father was grateful for the work but often had a frown when he came in from his job at the nursing home. At first, I thought it was the cold that had gotten to him, but as spring came and the weather changed, he still came into the house an unhappy man.

When Ted met with us and I interpreted for my father, I learned that the boss at the nursing home spoke unkindly to my father. He told me to explain to Ted that although he didn't know the words she was speaking, he knew that they were demeaning.

"Tell your father that this is a form of abuse, and it will not be tolerated," Ted said to me.

I relayed Ted's message, then listened to my father's reply.

"My father says it is important to honour the kindness of our sponsors, so he will continue to do the work at the nursing home," I said.

But Ted insisted there would be a change. And there was. Ted arranged for my father to leave the nursing home and helped him find other work.

After we spoke with Ted about the problem in the nursing home job—even though my father was still there for a bit— my father's frown began to fade. I hoped it was because he could see that our sponsors were dedicated to our happiness and well-being, and that his children—myself included— were building a life.

Chapter 26

Summer 1980

I wore my pale-blue, pompommed toque right into spring, which thawed the white world we lived in. The temperatures crept up to the point I could remove my toque, even though I didn't want to. By the summer, the house that could see the whole world began to distance itself from us, because we were pulling away from it. We needed to be in town more for part-time jobs, school, and to be around people. I thought that maybe deep in its soul, beyond the creaking floorboards and into its foundation, it had a calendar, and it knew its time of being set aside for us was coming to an end, even though we had not been there a year. I imagined it whispering to the barn that it would be watching us from its place on the hill where it could see the whole world, and I believe it did.

It was our first home, surrounded by fields that went on forever, and in the shelter of its Canadian arms, we had restarted our lives, a language, relationships with people who called us family, and a connection with a place that sustained us. But to be less isolated and more immersed in Canadian life, it was necessary to move into Uxbridge. I knew I needed and wanted to be closer to those people who had come into my life and be nearer to school. If I was in town, I could have a paper route or two or three, and I could take on extra jobs after school.

One of the few Asian families in town, Mr. and Mrs. Eng, owned a massive two-story house. Their children had moved away, and the two of them, senior citizens, poked around on the main floor. They decided that their second floor would be perfect for us to rent. It probably wasn't a coincidence that it was right across from the post office where Doris worked. They spoke Chinese too, which was especially helpful for my mom.

The house that could see the whole world must have laughed when it watched us try to squeeze into what was termed an apartment. Yet we did. It was plenty big enough. The nine of us managed reasonably well—goodness knows how our two landlords handled all the footsteps above them.

In Uxbridge, everything was close. I could walk my brothers and sisters to school. The post office was steps away, so it was easy to pick up our newspapers. On cold days, when my blue, pompommed toque worked together with a scarf in double duty, Doris Muckle drove us to our route so we didn't have to haul the heavy papers as we leaned into the arctic winds.

I was no longer isolated. I'd needed to be at first. I think we'd all needed to be so that we could breathe our first Canadian breaths in a protected space. We'd needed to decompress and process. We'd needed to dream within the sounds of our own family. From hut to house. From platform to beds. From Asian to English. From sandals to boots. The house on the hill, that house that could see the whole world, would forever be the house where I discovered a new life. I think it set us all up for life in town where we saw people every day, where we were required to blend, bend, stretch, and mix. Where we could be around people who we could lean on and learn from.

My father expanded his work world, finding work a long bus ride away, in Toronto, at a clothing store. He became their tailor, working for Dylex, a division of Tip Top Tailors. When he explained the finances to me, as he had when we'd been on the island, he told me he earned a small base salary and was paid by piecework. He pushed himself to do as much as possible. I thought it might be that being in Toronto brought him some peace in the way of feeling closer to his people—I knew from several trips into the city that Toronto's Chinatown covered a large area and was densely populated. He told me he'd met someone there who allowed him to sleep, each weeknight, on their kitchen floor. On the weekends, he returned by bus to Uxbridge.

My mother found a job in a restaurant, steps away from the apartment. Michael was introduced to the concept of being babysat by me and my eldest brother and sister, then daycare.

Two of my siblings and I got paper routes, delivering the *Toronto Star* after school and the *Globe and Mail* on weekends. We went canvassing and got more customers. I won the delivery-boy prize—there was a choice: a certain amount of money or an eight-track player. I chose the eight track, unsure if I could ever afford more than a couple of tapes.

But I was dedicated to working hard, and apparently my hard work was noticed. A family doctor, Dr. St. John, sent a letter to the newspaper saying I was the best paperboy they'd ever had. It was such an honour to hear this from a successful Canadian professional.

There were nine mouths to feed. We counted on one another to be breadwinners. We were, together, a complicated abacus with people on a wire instead of beads. With my father's meagre salary, my mother's income from the restaurant, bottle-picking money, paper route income, funds from shoveling the sidewalks of the CIBC bank, some fruit picking in the summer, and even plucking chickens, we got by without accumulating debt.

It wasn't easy. Or calm. Or perfect.

While we had lots of well-meaning supporters, not all my experiences with them were positive. One lady took me to a store called Stedman's and bought a pair of shoes for me. I remember they cost two dollars. Her kindness was genuine, and I was extremely grateful.

Weeks after she bought them for me, she saw me and discovered there were holes in their soles. I'd worn them through from all the walking on the paper routes. I could tell by the tone of her voice that she was angry with me—even if I couldn't understand the stream of words that she rained down over my bowed head. It was as if she thought I had abused the shoes. I wished Doris was there to speak the words I couldn't—to explain how much I appreciated the shoes. I wasn't sure how to respond. So, I kept my head low. I wanted to cry.

That small event cut me as if it had been a physical attack. I stood there on the sidewalk and felt like someone had stabbed me. In that moment, the shame filled me head to toe and lasted for a long time in every step I took.

There were a lot of arguments between our parents. Words tossed about in our first language that were steeped in doubt. "We should have stayed in Vietnam," or, "There's not enough money to feed us all," or, "If we had known it was going to be like this, maybe it would have been better under the regime." Or the one that stung, "We only came here because of you children." I made myself believe that it was their exhaustion speaking, the sum of all they'd been through: the fall of Saigon, the abandonment or collapse of my grandfather—not that he was responsible for the war, but his choices had bled into their have-tos and musts—the dangers on the boat and survival on the island and everything that followed. It was hard to hear their profound disappointment of having had children so they could help in the family business, only to end up with no business and all the children. There were many times when I heard those arguments and wished I'd never been born.

In those early days, there were many times our whole family was far away from Lao Tzu's peaceful world, but occasionally there was a shining moment—like when we were laughing together at something silly Michael would do or say.

I hardly heard from my grandfather—not in any inky letters, and not through his spirit. He was absent, and that created a sad space in me.

"You are safe in Canada," I imagined him whispering to me in my dreams. But I never did hear him say it.

"My parents sacrificed everything for my freedom," I said to him. There was nothing stopping me from sharing a message with him.

Every night, I collapsed on my bed, grateful for life, and relieved to rest my aching jaws from language gymnastics. And I'd fall asleep looking over at the hanging toque with the pale-blue pompom that made me look so much taller.

Chapter 27

Jamestown

Canada had been home to my family for over a year. Our sponsors were able to step back a little. My father worked long hours in Toronto. He'd talked about all the opportunities a city could offer a growing family, and then dropped into the conversation how he felt a connection to Toronto's Chinatown. Mostly, he was tired of travelling back and forth—my mother and Ted told me he had his eye on a second job, and a third, which he could organize if he didn't have to travel back every weekend.

I didn't want to leave Uxbridge. I'd gotten to know a few kids. I knew my way around the school. I was used to the teachers. I had my paper routes, and I knew where to find bottles. Ted had signed me up in soccer; I totally loved it. He was always there to cheer me on at games.

As preparations were made to leave the apartment—the second floor of the Eng's huge house—Doris, Ted, Barbara,

Lloyd, and Mary assured me that I was not gone from their lives. "We are family," said Barbara.

The subsidized rentals of the Ontario Housing Authority meant my family could live in Toronto, in the suburb of Jamestown. They provided a townhouse for which the rent was based on the family's income.

During the move, I continued to be my father's translator—rental agencies, school district in Toronto, whatever needed to be done in English, which, given we were in Canada, was everywhere—except Chinatown. The more I translated, the more my English vocabulary grew. I had better descriptions for concepts, I could summarize situations without sounding like a small child. I didn't carry my dictionary around with me as much.

Jamestown met the needs of low-income families. While it was not a ghetto, there was rusted junk outside many of the townhomes, and lots of places had tattered curtains at the windows that told me nothing had changed for a while and that places had been lived in by the same person for a long time. I didn't want to be a long-timer.

Jamestown felt like a whole other world. Uxbridge seemed a million miles away, even though it was only ninety minutes by car. Where there had been space in Uxbridge, there was none in Jamestown. Where there had been tranquility, there was chaos. I'd once felt safe; now I was fearful. Community was replaced by a kind of separation—people packed more closely together wanted to keep to themselves. It was simply too scary to trust. No one knew us. We knew no one. There was an unwritten rule of the survival kind that said: Keep it that way.

The only positive was that my father could now travel to and from his work with more ease. Because he was based in Toronto, he could find another job, or two, within the city—he sometimes worked three jobs. My mother found work too. My brother, sister, and I—the three eldest—attended school and found part-time work.

If there's one thing Jamestown's no-small-town-ness did for me, it was to force the innocence out of me that the charm and patience of Uxbridge had offered and nurtured. In doing so, Toronto, especially Jamestown, pushed me to communicate faster and become city savvy.

Chapter 28

Strawberry Fields

I STILL HAD MY CONNECTION to Uxbridge. Even though Ted and Barbara had their own large family, they continued to help me with my soccer games. I'd take the bus from Toronto to Scarborough, where Ted would meet me and drive me to Uxbridge. When my team played in tournaments, I'd stay at their home for the weekend.

One summer, my sister and brother and I were offered work in Uxbridge. We picked strawberries—two dollars a basket. Twenty dollars a day, usually. Hour after hour of work under the blistering sun. We'd make it a competition, we three eldest, to see who could earn the most. We'd stay longer and rake the grounds for the farmer. It was hard, hot work, but we did it. At the end of the day, we'd gather all the money together. It was family income, not personal income. Those were the summers we stayed with Doris Muckle. She'd drop us off at the farm, go to work at the post office, then pick us up after work and take us home. She'd always been single, but she was very good at caring, having been a nurse and then looking after her elderly parents. She seemed to enjoy three children appearing in her life for a summer.

It was great to be out in Uxbridge instead of in Jamestown. Clean air. I didn't have to keep looking over my shoulder when I took the bus or walked to the store or school. When September came around, I headed back to Jamestown and got my head stuck back in the books. I had to find another job to work after school and on weekends. Must succeed, high marks, excel, honours lists, work, go to Uxbridge, never stop. Carry the responsibility of translation.

I knew the details of our family's financial situation because, as the eldest, I was a stand-in for my father on the business part of things. It was just as it would have been were we still back in Vietnam with the textile business. My grandfather had deemed it to be that way.

The school years whizzed by. Grade six with Mrs. Dow and Mrs. Hagar, the math teacher the other kids said was mean but who had a soft spot for me because I loved numbers and was studious. The next moment, grade seven and then grade eight sailed by. Grade nine meant I'd change schools, which I did with more confidence than when we'd moved from Uxbridge. I was a willow, able to bend in any direction, depending on the situation. Me and my brothers and sisters walked in two worlds, east and west.

My language skills had improved, and I felt more confident with my vocabulary and far less self-conscious when trying out new words. I found myself switching from one of several Asian languages to English mid-sentence, mid-thought, and mid-dream. Toronto's ethnic diversity allowed me to blend in more than Uxbridge had. I began to see how this diversity was important for my parents' comfort. They, too, were more relaxed than they had been for some time. Jamestown had become familiar to my parents: the Chinese food place nearby, the street conversations with families that they'd managed to get to know, memorizing the bus routes. We'd take the bus to Chinatown to buy groceries. One time, my father and I were sitting at the back of the bus on the way home, and the whole wired and wheeled trolley tipped over, and our groceries spilled all over the aisle. We were slightly embarrassed when we scrambled to collect it all, but I didn't feel out of place. We'd ridden that bus hundreds of times. The people on it knew us and helped us gather what had fallen. I made some friends at school, but as other teens began to party, I went to work. My personal life was much different than most of the other students—more serious, incredibly focused, working to help keep my family fed and clothed. My father remained at his sewing job and then other jobs too. It seemed no one was ever home at the same time. There'd be a pot of rice on the stove for everyone to take their meals from.

And though we were all settling into the melting pot of Jamestown in Toronto, the community of Uxbridge continued to hold my hand, never letting go.

CHAPTER 29

The Houses That Ted Found

"YOU'VE GOT TO GET OUT of here." Ted Murphy stood in our subsidized Jamestown rental. He was concerned about the crime on the streets around the housing authority.

Ted was right. Jamestown was a rough neighbourhood when we moved in, but three years later, it had become a lot tougher, even dangerous. But there was something else Ted was concerned about.

The Ontario Housing Authority calculated monthly rent by making one week of income equal a month of rent. Ted said this policy kept poor people poor. "It is financially dysfunctional and oppressive," he explained.

I understood what he meant. It kept people in the same place in their financial situation because it didn't encourage people to make more money so they could save more. Twenty-five percent of someone's income sounds great for rent, but only when that income is above the poverty line. When a family income is extremely low, and the number of family members is greater than the average family, the costs for food and clothing and essentials take up a larger percentage of a small amount of money.

"Please, think about it," said Ted. "We need to find a way for you to buy a house before prices are out of reach."

It wasn't just prices that were out of reach. While we might be able to pay a mortgage payment by pooling together all of our earnings, there was no way for us to generate a down payment.

Ted never let up. He pushed and pushed for my parents to become homeowners. Although we were savers, with my mother, father, and me and the next two eldest working and going to school, we still had to provide food for nine mouths and clothing for us all. A house purchase was not in our stars.

And then, as I was ready to start school in the fall of 1984, Ted appeared again. He had found a place, right across from Humber College. It was five minutes away from where we lived—far enough away from the sketchy development we were in, but still close enough that my siblings' schools would not change. He told me to translate for my father that if my father didn't buy it then, he'd never get into the housing market.

"It is $89,000," said Ted.

I calculated. That amount was equal to 44,500 baskets of strawberries. A lifetime of summers could never produce that many baskets. My father was making $3.75 an hour. The mortgage interest rates were in the double digits. We couldn't swing it.

Ted was relentless—beautifully and generously so. He returned one week later to say he'd found another house—a similar price, similar location. As I began to translate my father's objection to him, that we just couldn't raise the down payment, he held out an envelope.

"There is this kind person who said she didn't want me to say who she was, but I think you know who she is," he said.

My father opened the envelope. There was a letter.

"I have enough for me. I'd rather you use this and succeed. I want to see you succeed.—Doris."

Folded inside the letter was a cheque.

The numbers and the letters equaled the same amount: $20,000.00. Twenty thousand dollars! It made my heart burst. I wanted to cry, but not with sadness.

Ted went on to explain that Doris did not need the money to be paid back.

"If we accept it, we will pay it back," said my father.

How could our family accept the equivalent of 10,000 baskets of strawberries? There was a protective boundary around my father's independence, and he had instilled it in me. We'd been gifted a life in Canada. Thank you. We could provide for ourselves, and we would.

Ted wouldn't let go. He shared how there is a balance between receiving and giving. He pushed. And then he pushed some more. That was Ted.

Community. Family. Kindness. That was Uxbridge. That was Canada.

As the sale proceeded, Ted asked me to meet with a lawyer to make sure there was no lien against the property. I did as Ted asked.

I sat in the waiting room for a little while. Then a well-dressed man came through the door of an inner office. He looked around and called out, "Mr. Banh?"

I stood.

The man's jaw dropped. "You're just a kid," he said.

He was right, I'd ridden my bike over from school during lunchtime.

Once I explained that Ted sent me, his attitude changed.

Ted later told me that he could have made a call, but he wanted me to understand how to buy a house.

Our new house had enough bedrooms for my parents to have their own. There was room for us four boys to be in one room, another for the three girls, plus my mother's mother when she came to stay for a while until she could no longer stay away from her beloved Vietnam.

My father sponsored other relatives, and they stayed with us too. Over the years, the house almost burst at the seams—perhaps it didn't because my parents were tailors. It might be they stayed up all night sewing patches over its tears and reinforcing its corners. Maybe it didn't burst because, between school and work, not everyone was ever in the house at one time, and people like my father were rarely there at all.

Our address changed, but my role remained the same. My father would still have me take time off school when he went to the immigration office as he inquired about sponsoring more family from Vietnam. He'd get frustrated with me at times, wanting me to translate different answers than the ones we were being given. I could only translate what was spoken to me, but sometimes, when I didn't agree with his reasoning, I'd choose to restate his requests to English-speaking clerks and keep the conversational sea as calm as possible. I was just as frustrated as he was.

I often wondered, *Why me? It's not my fault that you have so many kids.* Though I was frustrated with the role, I recognized it helped me as well as my father. If I hadn't been his translator, I wouldn't have gotten as close to all our sponsors, people who were like extra parents and grandparents to me. Being his translator allowed me to communicate better in an adult world and to be more diplomatic.

Sometimes, when a breeze came in through the window of the bedroom I slept in with my brothers, and I was awake enough to notice, I'd turn and think that my grandfather might be whispering to me, but he never did. It was like his spirit had cut off our conversations. I wondered if he had stopped being able to teach, or if I had learned the basics and was doing okay on my own.

My grandfather's lessons of the past remained with me, but I had witnessed his physical person, his emotional body, change after the fall of Saigon. Then he went to Hong Kong. My father has told me there was a long stretch, when we were refugees, during which my grandfather didn't even know if we were alive.

The purchase of the home grounded me more in being Canadian. I was so proud of all of us—and it showed in my enthusiasm to work hard at school and at my part-time jobs. Even though we'd been in Canada for a few years, I was still amazed I had a bed, clothing, a schoolbag, books, teachers who were interested in sharing their gift, and sponsors who would not let us go even though we were now in Toronto, even though they had fulfilled their agreement to help us.

Ted and Barbara, Doris, and Lloyd and Mary helped me learn to use my negative feelings as a mirror, and along with those early-in-life lessons from my grandfather, I was able to learn the art of reframing issues with gratitude, tolerance, patience, and compassion.

Chapter 30

Endings

WE WERE GOING ABOUT OUR daily routines when my father came to me and told me that my grandmother had passed away in Hong Kong, and that since then my grandfather had become even sadder. "He cannot find the peace he once knew," said my father.

Even though my grandfather was living with his youngest daughter, and she was married with two children that he could have shared his wisdom with, as he had me, he could not adjust. "He is in a state of anguish," said my father. "I have asked him to come to Canada to be with us."

When my grandfather arrived from the airport, there was no life in his eyes. He turned away from conversations, not into them as he had been when we were together in Vietnam. It would have been a shock for people to learn that I was once his golden boy. I did not know what to say to him. And he rarely spoke to me. As a teenager, busy with school and a job, I wasn't around much, which suited me because it was painful to see him under such a dark cloud. It was hard to believe this was the grandfather of my childhood. He reminded me of the man I'd seen sitting at the base of a tree on Air Raya, the one who was gone the next morning.

Though my grandfather's entrepreneurial spirit was alive in me, it had long departed him. He was sad. He came with some illnesses inside him, and he developed more while he was with us, including diabetes. He lost weight. Grief had taken hold of every cell. He'd lost his business, his city, and now his wife. He had many regrets and voiced them in low tones.

Now there were thirteen of us living in the house: my uncle, another relative I didn't know, my parents, seven kids, my father's father, and my mother's mother.

My mother's mother and my father's father were opposites. My mother's mother was always smiling. She said so little yet displayed so much gratitude and happiness, despite missing her sons and grandsons. I was grateful she was there to at least try to brighten my grandfather's days—to keep him company and bring a sense of elders-from-the-east into his life and our home. Eventually, she decided to return to Vietnam because she missed it so much, and she later passed when she was in her nineties.

But my grandmother's good nature was not enough for my grandfather to find peace. The body reflects the spirit, and his diabetes became worse. Soon he was hospitalized.

One day, I spotted my father outside my classroom. I knew that meant my grandfather had passed away. I helped my father translate at the hospital. Then he dealt with arranging a full Chinese funeral. A Buddhist monk, the burning of incense, and the appropriate prayers were all part of the service that honoured my grandfather's life.

I held my fond memories to my heart and watched my father as he stood in his own private reflection. "I am proud of you, Father," I whispered in the direction of my father. I swallowed. I breathed. Somewhere inside me I moved toward a death-is-not-death mindset. I decided I would not grieve. I would honour, revere, and respect. I believed my grandfather had done enough grieving for all of us.

"Goodbye for now," I told my grandfather when I went to sleep that night. I hoped he had found peace and that he would message me. There was not even the slightest breeze.

In our busy lives as earners and learners, the one constant was working hard. I worked the 3:30 p.m. to 1:30 a.m. shift every Friday, Saturday, and Sunday at a Toronto plastics factory that operated 24/7—thirty hours of work squeezed in between school weeks. Saturday, Sundays, and holidays meant I got paid double time, which was $7.00 an hour. I worked every holiday shift I could, including Christmas Day.

I didn't really need additional motivation, but I chose to focus on the balance of the double-digit interest mortgage on the house, Doris's loan, and savings for my university education. My grandfather's long-ago shared wisdom echoed in my head: Every person has the same number of hours in a day, and there's only so much a person can earn an hour. He'd explained in simple terms the concept of having one's money working for them so that the earnings generated a return above and beyond the limited exchange of an hour for a dollar.

My plan was to invest in a good education so that I would be able to get my money working for me, to generate more than whatever I could earn through a salary. That was where I set my sights—not on having fun, dating, and partying.

I was also driven to save money, which was difficult with so many demands and earning so little. But contemplating a return to the poverty we'd experienced on that island in the South China Sea was terrifying. I could not allow that to happen.

And then circumstances threw a wrench into my plans. The work in the factory was monotonous, and it was too easy to not pay attention. When I sliced my finger, rather seriously, on a machine, the owners expected me to return to work immediately. That lack of concern combined with the fear that I'd injure myself again, perhaps worse next time, gave me the courage to walk away. And it fueled the motivation for a higher education. I felt that this would put me in a position where I could positively change working conditions for people.

I trusted there were other jobs and that someone was always hiring. One of those people was Ted. His accounting office was in Scarborough. I worked the summers of grade ten and eleven for him. That was when he introduced me to golf. I did not like it at all when I started. I couldn't hit the ball! Ted just laughed and said I'd come to love the game.

My father and I sat across from the bank manager and proceeded to cause quite the stir. The teenager, me, did all the talking for the two of us.

"You want to renew or renegotiate your mortgage?" asked the bank representative.

"No, sir. We are here to pay it off," I said, slowly and clearly. The bank manager was confused by the fact that I, the teenager, was doing all the talking. Then he thought I was making a mistake with my English, which, while better, was still clearly not my mother tongue.

I repeated the sentence as if English was *his* second language.

His face relaxed out of its squint, and his frown morphed into a head-tilting combination of shock and respect. We had worked hard, every one of us in the family, and managed to save enough to pay off the mortgage within five years. Our culture dictated no debt. We were intent on honouring that.

With the mortgage out of the way, the next step was Doris's $20,000. We paid it back in full, accompanied by our eternal gratitude. And our focus then turned to school funds.

Chapter 31

Graduations and Growing Up

Our high school was sponsoring a trip to Europe, but I dismissed it because there wasn't room in my budget after pay-the-mortgage, repay-Doris, and save-for-university. But it was Doris who insisted I go, and that she wanted to invest in my success. She said her life experience gave her a wider view of my future than I could see. And Doris always got what she wanted.

Her generosity and her investment in me and others helped me see the world from a wider perspective—physically and spiritually. I had to accept the trip to Europe and accept that I didn't need to feel guilt that I wouldn't be working when I was travelling. I had to tell myself I was not letting my family down by taking the trip. It planted the travelling seed in me—travel for pleasure, not for survival in the way our travel from Vietnam to Canada had been. I knew I had to travel more in the future.

Before graduation, I was chosen as valedictorian.

Though I had the second highest marks in the class, the distinction was decided by other students in a nomination-of-peers system. Some teachers voiced doubts that I'd be able to deliver a valedictorian speech, given English was my second language. Still, they awarded me the honour.

My nervousness was intense. I couldn't sleep. I couldn't focus. I went to the doctor and told him I didn't think I could do it. When I told him how scared I was, Dr. Tam took me out of the examination room and into the hallway. Once we were out of his office, he led me down a hallway. Confused, I followed him to a locked door. Once he'd unlocked it, he asked me to step inside his supply room, then pointed to a box on the floor.

"That whole box is filled with valium," he said. He explained what valium was—a chemical that suppresses fear and induces relaxation. "I could prescribe that for you, but here's another idea. Go home. Write your speech. Practice until you can say it all without looking at the page. Practice over and over."

I went home and sat down to compose the speech. From deep inside, the little boy in me told me to prove that I was good enough, and to silence the doubts of the teachers. I wrote the speech and I practiced it over and over and over and over . . .

Dr. Tam gave me the opportunity to look at my fear and move forward in the face of it. I chose to speak anecdotally rather than go into academics. Each time I practiced, my voice was freer and more natural than the time before. I began to know the speech inside and out. My voice relaxed as I repeated stories of the events and school happenings. When I didn't need the pages anymore, I still felt that they were part of me.

The day came for me to deliver the speech. As I stepped up to the podium, my heart connected with every person in the auditorium. I looked out at the audience and, though I couldn't see everyone, I knew that Doris, Ted, Barbara, Lloyd, and Mary were sitting on either side of my parents—I knew all my Uxbridge family was there.

The teachers had been worried I couldn't do it. I had been worried I couldn't do it. But I did it. I found myself at the end of the speech facing an auditorium full of people on their feet. A standing ovation! Their applause was like thunder. It validated the hard work I had put in. I was deeply proud of myself. It gave me the confidence to know I could speak any time I was asked in the future. My high school career finished at a high point.

I believe the spirit of my grandfather watched from a place where all those who have passed celebrate the part of creation known as life. Maybe even the house that could see the whole world was watching.

In my dreams that night, I might have dreamed that it was a dragon that delivered the speech. *"Perhaps you are the dragon,"* whispered Vietnam.

"Maybe you're an elephant," said another part of the world I could not quite make out.

"You are enough," said Canada.

"I am still a boy," I said in my sleep.

A dragon. An elephant. Enough. A boy. I rolled over and wondered if we are all shape-shifters when we need to be.

I graduated in the spring of 1988, worked the summer, and was ready for university in the fall. It was time for me to leave the house in Toronto. My parents were settled. My siblings were in school, each of them with university plans of their own. I'd been accepted to McMaster University in Hamilton, Ontario. I had scholarships for being an honour student, though my planning, frugality, and independence made it so I did not use all of them.

My goal of becoming a doctor was a little closer. From valedictorian to university entrant—my mind went back to the leg injury, the American dollar bill covering the wound, the doctor, and the seed his message had planted. "You're going to be just fine—now," he had said.

I was fine. Now.

Chapter 32

The Bridge between Two Lives

I ARRIVED AT UNIVERSITY ALL set for academic study, thanks to scholarships and savings. But I felt far from worry-free. I was holding my head above water, against the pressure and guilt of having left the house and my father when he had been used to me handling so much. I pushed that pressure from home into a tiny space deep within. I needed to concentrate on my future.

All around me was a sea of youth excited about their first year of university. I wanted some of that youthful exuberance. I was sixty in my head—a father figure. I was eighty in my body—worn out from physical labour. Rarely had I relaxed. Even when playing soccer or golf, it was always sandwiched between work, school, and transport. The world may have been full of possibility, but I saw only that which the island had imprinted on me: "Get an education, don't be poor, be a doctor." There was no other option, and no in-between.

As the "Song of the Witches" in Shakespeare's *Macbeth* begins, "Double, double toil and trouble." I knew about toil—hard work was my life. There was a witch present. There had to have been a spell cast. Why else, when I was just starting my first day at McMaster University, on my own, did I not feel any freer than when I'd been working at a factory and in junior high? Why couldn't I feel unburdened? And I still had to pee all the time, the anxiety over the logistics of needing to know where the bathroom was making the urge even worse.

When I entered the tiny dorm room, a massive guy was sitting in the corner. I wondered how we'd manage in such a tiny space.

"It's okay," he said as if reading my mind. He had a soft, musical voice, and there was laughter in his words. "I'm Bill, your roommate's best friend. Cory wants you to know he'll be here in a few days."

I spent three days alone in a dorm room that was meant to be shared and aged a decade. I worried for my father. I worried for my mother. I worried for my siblings. How could I let go and trust they would all be okay after so many years of me managing the household and translating everything for my parents?

Then on the third day, after chasing my way across campus to find things I needed and checking in with my parents for something they needed, I let myself into the dorm room and froze. There, sitting on the edge of the bed meant for my roommate, was a life-size fluffy toy. The toy moved. My jaw dropped.

"Why are you so serious?" asked the gigantic, fluffy, living, breathing toy.

Suddenly, I was five years old. A real five-year-old, a Canadian five-year-old at that. My roommate, Cory, had arrived. Apparently, Cory had a part-time job as a mascot—he worked at the Canadian National Exhibition but never passed up an opportunity to be in character. When we became roommates, he thought it would be fun to dress up and wait for me to arrive.

When you share a tiny space with a guy with a big personality who likes to dress up in costumes, how can life not change?

"I'll go get us some food," said the mascot. And off he went in the Mercedes his father had bought for his recent nineteenth birthday.

Cory was a rulebreaker. He was nothing like me. He was the kid I'd never been. Over our time together, he gifted me precious things like ice-cream-dripping-down-your-arm, cheer-out-loud, laugh-until-you-are-doubled-over kind of fun. It was about time. Just as I was becoming an adult, I was learning how to be a kid.

One time, in the middle of the night, I woke doubled over, but not from fun. Cory rushed me to the hospital. They sent me home saying it was gas. But Cory did not leave me alone, and he took me back a few hours later. Appendicitis. Emergency surgery.

Cory cared about me. He was crazy caring. He was crazy fun. A mascot for life. He'd study all night—caffeine pills in a glow-in-the-dark costume.

Cory was my prescription for seeing fun and having fun. He brought the laughing Buddha to my heart.

Chapter 33

Gateway to Giving

During my first year at McMaster, a letter arrived from a lawyer. I was a little nervous in case it was some bad news. Mrs. Smith was a friend of Doris's who I'd met years before. She had left me $3,000 in her will. She wrote me a letter that said in her six decades of teaching, she'd never seen a child work so hard. Her recognition meant the world to me. If I ever doubted whether I was contributing to my family or helping my parents, I could reflect on her words.

During that first year, I began to ask myself what I could offer the world as a doctor. Where and how could I best serve? I had been a witness to many ways of the world. I had seen things I never wanted to see again but that allowed me to envision a better world. I knew that science and wonder were compatible. That we were still learning about the energy woven into the anatomical magic that comprises each human being. My heart stepped in, assembling the past and present and future, and it updated my perspective. The way I saw the world had evolved.

My heart handed me a word: vision.

I asked if I could shadow Dr. Chatoo, an eye doctor I knew. The experience changed my trajectory, and I decided to pursue optometry. Something inside me knew that the enlightened lens was so much more than the eyes and the brain; vision had to include the heart and the soul.

There was a long line of applicants for the optometry program at Waterloo, but I applied. During the interview with Dr. Lyle, I found out we shared a history with Uxbridge. He told me that he had lived in Leasdale, a subdivision of Uxbridge, and we chatted about the area. I told him how grateful I was for my Canadian family of sponsors who had helped me so much since arriving from Vietnam.

On June 2, 1992, I received a phone call. I figured Karma must have called Dr. Lyle or he called Karma. I could have danced down the street.

Before I knew it, I was attending the University of Waterloo, where I met many wonderful people, and where close and long-term friendships were born: Stelios—bold to my shy—was a popular, outgoing guy whose philosophy aligned with mine. Areef, a student two years ahead of me, brought a calming sageness to our interactions. Yih Ling seemed to complete my friend and study circle.

I like to think I was a little less serious by then, but it's true I applied myself to diligent study, leaving little time for anything else. I checked in with family, and Yih Ling and I became great friends. By the third year, I was part of the class doing rounds in the hospital, applying in the wards what I'd been learning in the lecture halls.

Some days, I felt like I'd been at school forever and that I would be in school forever. I needed a wake-up call, and that is what I got on rounds with Dr. Lisa Prokopich, who caught me during a period when I felt uninspired.

"What is wrong with this woman's eyes?" she asked, handing me a hand-held slit lamp, which is a special kind of microscope that allows us to see what's going on with a person's cornea, iris, vitreous, and retina. I peered into the lamp, but I couldn't tell her what was wrong, so I did not answer. She asked the question again to others. No one spoke. She asked a third time, this time looking back at me.

"I don't know," I said.

"You don't know?" her voice thundered through the silence. "Go home. You don't know shit."

My body shook. No teacher had ever said anything like that to me. I was the diligent, hardworking student who always excelled at academics! *How would I continue in my education? Would she dismiss me? Would the registrar's office strike me from the student list?*

My mind caught up with my feet once I'd left the building. She was right. I knew nothing. Or almost nothing. I had begun to fade. I'd been going to lectures but not reading as much as I should. I'd always been the numbers person, not the words guy.

Complacency had lulled me into thinking I was a great student. But I wasn't a complete student.

That day, I began to read. Truly read. I imagined the stories and patients around the words. If Cory had been my entry into understanding what it is like to have childlike fun, Dr. Lisa Prokopich was my gateway to deep learning through the written word.

Complacency lifted. My confidence improved, as did my commitment to my role as a student, to my future career, and to being a human who wanted to serve others.

With Dr. Prokopich over my shoulder as an invisible tutor, I pushed further.

I became closer to my study partner and friend, Yih Ling. We were also among a group of four students selected to go overseas and work at an eye clinic in Jamaica in the summer of 1995. The clinic had been set up by a native Jamaican who wanted to help the poorest of the poor. When I arrived, I was immediately taken back to the climate of Vietnam, as well as the poverty I'd seen as a refugee. The airport shack was without a roof. Customs would not let us pass because we had forgotten the document identifying us as volunteers, which meant the medical supplies we had with us were illegal. We waited for three hours until they had cleared it with the school.

It was a drought year for Jamaica, and water was rationed. There was no water available at the clinic, only a few fans worked, and we were sweating all the time. Examinations were difficult. But I remembered what I had learned so long ago on the island of Air Raya: "Give a person a fish, that is one meal. Teach a person to fish, their table is full for a lifetime." We were giving each person the gift of clearer vision so they could better witness and participate in their own journey.

Those who came for treatment had often endured a two-hour bus ride just to get to us. Many would ask us for money to take a taxi home. Their poverty was part of their journey and a part of mine. We were doing as much as we could with their diseased eyes, and we couldn't do much more. It was heart-wrenching.

Yih Ling and I became a couple that summer. Our shared commitment to hard work and the ease with which we travelled together helped us through our busy schedules.

I was a different student when I returned from Jamaica. I was more focused. I was ready to step beyond the excellent research that Waterloo offered, and I started to look to larger centres in the United States with the population to support practical study and hands-on experiences. The Omni Eye Center in Atlanta, Georgia, was offering an internship. Dr. Leff and Dr. Ajamian were the two main doctors who connected with us students.

When I was chosen, I was excited and scared because I'd heard that the doctors there were excessively strict. My intuition told me to go for it.

It turned out that Dr. Leff was a retinal specialist from Toronto who practiced in the States. He was so funny! He kept telling me I could earn more in the States in one month than I could earn in Canada in a year. Dr. Leff became a mentor to me and invited me to watch him perform surgery. I met him at five in the morning and witnessed a delicate surgery on a retinal detachment. He was at ease the entire time, joking while his hands flew about. Dr. Leff was a living example of someone listening to his heart and loving what he did.

Dr. Ajamian appeared to be a tough person, but his goal was simply to make sure we learned. His dedication to new students was incredible. He taught me to pay attention to what was happening and to let go of the ego. "When someone complains about the right eye, check the left eye," he said, because the obvious is not often the answer.

People are used to dealing with symptoms, but he taught me to look for the cause.

Chapter 34

Roadblocks

I HAD A JOB LINED up with a Dr. Ng in Toronto that would start after Waterloo and as soon as I had my license—one exam away. My marks were high. I loved my chosen science, and my career was a glittering beacon in front of me. It was all rolling along as planned.

Until it wasn't.

I wrote the exam. I failed.

How could it be that I failed?

My world came crashing down on me, bringing shame, embarrassment, confusion, and frustration. My job at risk, my career at risk, my self-confidence and my ego beaten and bruised.

I discovered many of my peers had failed too. One-third of the class had failed. Never had so many people sitting for this exam failed it. We were all excellent students.

I felt shame that I'd failed. And then I became angry.

There were politics, arrogance, and power involved. We discovered that the examination board had instituted a new exam, and there were irregularities in the administration of the test procedure. My friend Stelios stepped forward and helped me prepare a written complaint. It was pointed out to me that by the time any appeals were heard, we'd already be sitting for the exam again, since we could rewrite six months from the original test.

My heart said to take my energy elsewhere.

Dr. Ng showed compassion and understanding and assured me I still had a job. He proposed that, while Yih Ling covered for me at his clinic, I take a series of motivational tapes he had used in his career and occupy myself with them until I could rewrite in six months.

"You'll learn all about marketing and confidence," he said.

Dr. Ng rolled with the situation. Others were moving on too. The only one who seemed to be ashamed and angry was me.

I took a tutoring job in Forest Hill, a posh neighbourhood north of downtown Toronto. When I wasn't tutoring, I listened to the sales tapes that featured Brian Tracey. The time I spent listening to these lessons was one of the most productive six months of my life. The motivational instruction allowed me to understand marketing, sales, communication, dedication to the customer, and the value of a positive attitude. I could never have learned so much valuable information had I not had to wait to rewrite the exam. The shame of perceived failure was slowly replaced with a sense of confidence and appreciation. My heart took on a new view: Where there is no failure, there is no life.

Chapter 35

Fast-Forward, Return Home, Restart: 1997–2013

ONE YEAR WENT BY AS if it was a month. License in hand after that rewrite, I worked as many shifts for Dr. Ng as he needed me to because I wanted to thank him. It was all a blur.

The next time I caught myself in the life mirror, Yih Ling and I each had our own practices. Work was going well. When we weren't working, we'd regenerate by travelling far and wide, including Europe, the Galapagos, and my former homeland of Vietnam, which appeared both familiar and foreign at the same time.

Yih Ling and I were connected by our curiosity about the world. We had been dedicated students, then hardworking professionals and compatible travelling companions. Each of the countries we visited opened our eyes in new ways. At times, we were awestruck by architecture and the stories it told about the culture and the often backbreaking work performed mostly by those who were indentured, or even enslaved, to those with a powerful hand in dictating a class system. Yet the art and skill in the very walls, and in the spaces those walls surrounded, was breathtaking.

The natural areas of outstanding beauty, as in Africa and the Galapagos, were soul-stirring.

At times, I was so moved when I saw ancient buildings that I felt I once might have been there as a carpenter, a teacher, a scribe, or a starving peasant. Travels included two trips to Vietnam. The first was eye-opening for me; everything seemed so much smaller, worn, and primitive than I remembered it as a boy.

It was a rich, full life.

"Is this too good to be true?" I would sometimes ask myself. And then I would wake up in the middle of the night. "You don't know your own truth—yet," I would whisper to myself.

What I also began to see in the mirror was someone still looking for a home.

"I've got a plan," Courage said.

"I think I know what it is," I said.

"Then do it. Go home and practice optometry," said Courage.

Suddenly, I was inspired to look up the meaning of the word "doctor."

In Latin, "docere" means teacher. That was me—is me. Like Dr. Tam had done to me by taking me to the storage room to show me the boxes of valium, I spent extra time with my patients explaining all aspects of the situation with their vision.

"It's time to go back to Uxbridge," I said to myself. That was the easy part. When I shared my news with peers, they said I was crazy. Some said the money is in Toronto. Heads were shaken. Small town was mentioned. None of those statements meant anything to me.

I talked to Barbara and Doris about it. They reminded me to trust my heart. So, I moved my practice to Uxbridge and made plans to make my home there.

Chapter 36

Send in the Signs

In 2008, Ted Murphy passed. I leaned on my memories of him. I never wanted him forgotten. I arranged two annual scholarships for Uxbridge high school students in his honour. I called them the Ted Murphy Awards. I read all the essays, though the applicants were anonymous until after selection. One particular year, one of the scholarship recipients was Jennifer Murphy, a great-niece of Ted's. I marvelled how Ted's goodness was coming full circle.

Stelios and Areef, from university, reentered my life. We had all become doctors, we each had our own practices in and around Toronto, and we shared a deep interest in personal and professional development and inner peace as the foundation for happiness. When we got together, there was an instant depth and width. There was peace, a knowing, a bond. There was the brotherly love that says, "I've got your back."

We referred to ourselves as the BAG Brothers, of course—Buddha, Aristotle, Gandhi. We didn't search for those nicknames either, especially since Aristotle was on Stelios's birth certificate. We were the perfect first line of a cheesy joke—Aristotle, Buddha, and Gandhi went into a bar—there was no joke, but there was a lot of laughter.

We attended personal development seminars together, set goals, grew when we didn't even know we were growing, and supported each other through life's surprises, sorrow, joy, and struggle. Stelios, Areef, and I became hungry for more growth. The courses we attended made us yearn for more knowledge, and our regular meetings would last for hours in a coffee shop, then continue in the parking lot.

We became serious about life and love in a way that embraced side-splitting humour—often we would laugh at ourselves. And we could grieve, forgive, embrace, and know that, just as there are no stupid questions, there are no wrong answers. We laughed about the fact that people in our lives noticed the difference in our energy.

"What an amazing life," Uxbridge said to me one night in my dreams.

My pleasure to give back expanded. There were charity events and sponsorships of others. Being back in Uxbridge meant the world to me. My connections with others grew deeper. My youngest brother, Michael, had become a dentist. We became part of a health centre—a community.

When I stopped to take stock, sixteen years had passed since I had become an eye doctor. I couldn't account for them all. If it wasn't for the photos of the dozens of countries I'd visited, I'd have thought the calendar was tricking me.

But behind the scenes of an incredible life, there had been another sixteen years of frustration and confusion and anxiety over my bladder issue. Something was not normal.

I continued to be hugely inconvenienced by my bladder. In airport lineups, my travelling companion would hold my place in line while I visited the washroom multiple times. When travelling alone, I simply lost my place in line. On some trips, I tried not drinking liquids for so long that I began to feel ill from dehydration, but even that didn't work. I still needed to go. I returned to medical practitioners time and again, but there was no help to be had. Specialists could find nothing wrong.

There was the stress of the near-constant physical urge, of course. But I was ashamed, exhausted from carrying the heavy weight of my secret, and I felt defeated from not being able to solve it.

Courage once again tapped my shoulder, and I decided to share with Stelios and Areef my struggle with the unworthiness and shame that was connected to what I could only call "the bathroom issue."

Once I'd shared, a huge weight was removed from my shoulders. I'd told two people and the world had not ended. I realized that even though I still had to figure out how to handle the problem, I was no longer weighed down by the secretive part of it.

"Secrets are exhausting," I said to my BAG brothers.

"Not anymore," they said.

I went home to talk with my inner self.

"Notice that life will not end when you share a deep secret with someone you trust," said my inner self.

Sharing, in fact, became the foundation for moving past fear. I found more room for more courage, and my desire to give back grew even bigger.

"I want to transform the world for one million people," I said to Areef and Stelios. "No, wait. One billion."

They didn't even flinch. They just nodded that kind of supportive nod that said, "Of course you do. You're already on your way."

I whispered my billion-people wish to the wind as if I was holding the stem of a dandelion puff of white seeds, and I imagined my words were being carried away by the breeze and taken to a place where they would be dealt with by a higher power. This left me lighter.

Chapter 37

Africa Speaks

I WAS OVERCOME BY THE magnificence of the African continent, a giant geographical vessel holding the wildest of the wild, and the most complex political and cultural challenges—all so fragile within such a vast expanse. And such sacredness: the birthplace of mankind. Every breath was a lesson in human history. Regardless of ethnic labels today, Africa had watched us leave, epic era after era, to inhabit the world.

I'd like to believe anyone who travels to Africa as a tourist turns into a wonder-filled observer, a revere-er of life, and a student of conservation, and returns home humbler than when they left. I was oohing and ahhing over the majesty of animals and swallowing the lump in my throat over the heartbreaking realities of their tenuous connection to life. As I stared out at a stand of trees, I'm sure I looked every part the tourist living out a dream to safari. A breeze stirred my gratitude for being present.

"Cheers, mate," said an Aussie accent from behind me. "You come all the way from Hong Kong?"

Ordinarily, I'd go into a logistical, ancestral, and immigrational explainer: My grandparents walking from China to Vietnam, Vietnam to—well—with my parents and siblings on the open ocean, from the open ocean to a deserted tropical island, from that first island to another island, from that island to Edmonton and then Toronto, Canada, then to the nearby town of Uxbridge where I live and have my optometry practice.

Instead, I wanted to say, "Sir, we are all from Here." Yet I held off, because I did not know whether to stretch out my arms and gesture HERE, as in the glorious savanna, or if I should hold my hands here, to my heart.

Perhaps they are the same place.

Africa had turned me into a wonder-filled observer and revere-er of life, as well as a student of conservation, and made me humbler than when I'd arrived. Being present at an elephant sanctuary, where I witnessed the goodness of rescuers who had transformed a situation that had arisen from poaching, allowed me to start seeing even more connections. Africa raised my consciousness through a community of brothers and sisters—human, animal, plant, and what we call inanimate—but what we call a thing or inanimate is not: A mountain is alive, a rock is energy, soil contains riches that are made of life and death itself.

But I was, after all, still a tourist. Enter the gift shop—literally.

On my first day inside the shop, I'd seen a group of small, carved elephants in the window. Twelve of them. Each day, as I passed the shop's window, they called to me. Why, when I'm not a souvenir kind of guy?

But something came over me. A landslide of an idea.

"I'll take them all," I said to the clerk.

"All the elephants?"

"All the elephants," I replied.

"Twelve elephants," said a dragon. I looked around; there was no one there but me and the salesperson.

Because elephants travel over great distances, they play a key role as builders and conservationists, carrying tree seedlings within their massive bodies, transplanting them far and wide. Scientists have documented lower tree diversity, which creates a less healthy and less resilient forest, in areas that have lost elephants. Where elephants are still present, many communities have launched antipoaching initiatives, which makes those communities safer and more secure than before.

As one of the women in a village said about the elephants being safe and the rebels gone, "I can take my shoes off at night."

Twelve. Why had I bought twelve? The twelve elephants were all the hours in the day, the hours in the night, the months in the year, the apostles in the Christian world—the twelve elephants were the sum of all humanity.

I found a shady place to sit. Maybe, I thought, the sun had gotten to me.

Intuition, Curiosity's life partner, spoke to me then. My true heart speaking. An intelligence beyond book learning. I stopped questioning the why of the elephants and, once in my pocket, they stirred impatiently.

Then I realized there were twelve individuals who had stepped into my life before I even knew they had—the sponsors whose benevolence had altered the course of my life, and the kind people who taught me many lessons: Michael McLuhan, Barbara and Ted Murphy, Lloyd and Mary Ball, Doris Muckle, Lorne and Margaret Wall, Nelson Cheung, John Wilson, and John and Carol Fowles.

In that moment, I knew I would not keep any of the elephants. I would give one to each of these game-changers in my life as a talisman, a way to remind them of their talents and gifts. And the elephant would become a symbol of a request: that they share their gifts with others to create a ripple effect of goodness. The twelve elephants were symbols that represented those who had helped me, and the elephants represented those who would help others. They became my way to multiply the good deeds done and the good deeds yet to do.

On my return to Canada, each of these changemakers, these ambassadors of goodness, appeared promptly on my return to Canada, as if curated. And they became recipients.

It was because of the long-lasting gift I received through the kindness and generosity of my twelve elephant-recipients that I could take my shoes off at night, resting easy and sleeping barefoot.

Chapter 38

Endings as Beginnings

Yih Ling and I had grown together. We'd nurtured each other in the early years to encourage confidence as we found our way. We'd found a fast-paced, satisfying rhythm together, each working many, many hours in our respective practices—by choice.

Then, suddenly, we had grown apart. Our ways were different.

I became frustrated with myself and my complacency— my tendency to let things move along and assume they were going well. I never realized that check-ins, relationship maintenance, and up-front discussions about even small differences of opinion were necessary.

I kept telling myself that endings are beginnings. I told myself that if the start of a relationship is a catalyst for growth, then the end of a relationship is a recognition of that growth, a re-evaluation of the journey, and an opportunity for the highest self to accept the parting.

It was going to be okay. Painful, yes. I convinced myself it could be peaceful pain.

My separation from Yih Ling was more stoic than peaceful. It affected me deeply, of course. Yet it impacted me the way a fish might break the surface of a pond to see the sky more clearly than from its home under the water.

The value of reframing events, like ends as beginnings, became relevant as I became more focused on my energy and how I allowed the energy of others to affect me. I had work to do to ensure more two-way joyful connections. I had taught others how to treat me. Family members knew they could rely on me, and I went the extra mile without expecting anything from anyone. Which was fine.

But I didn't consider the effect on me. I found it hard to say no even when I knew saying yes would create turmoil inside, or put me in a difficult situation, or exhaust me. I thought peace meant doing what other people said I should do.

As I entered this new phase of spiritual growing and getting to know my true self, I played more golf and amped up my running because they brought me peace of mind.

I discovered that, when running marathons, many people don't wear the correct shoes. I became obsessed with researching and trying and buying running shoes in a bid to perform better and reduce injury risk.

Then I discovered chi running, which focuses on a strong core. With the body relaxed, using the core for the power, impact injuries are reduced and recovery after a run is much quicker. Chi running relies on technique versus dependency on shoe design. This technique helped me to heal my body physically from having worn the wrong shoes.

My resting heart rate dropped dramatically, and the sense of health and well-being I experienced was intense. I realize, looking back, that I had stopped running away from life and had changed direction to run toward something greater: consciousness, more love, and a kind of freedom. This freedom began to manifest itself in me becoming a better listener, being open to new concepts, and flowing with life rather than against it.

I was so overjoyed with my results that I wanted other people to enjoy the experience of chi running as much as I did. (Plus, I secretly admitted, it would help me meet others.) I began informally coaching people in the chi method.

The thing is, I kept buying running shoes. One day, I realized that I had closets full of them. Suddenly I was back on the sidewalk in Uxbridge, a little boy with newspapers in his arms, while a lady shouted words he didn't understand about how she had only just bought him the shoes he was wearing, and they were already worn out.

In her heart of hearts, I am certain she didn't want to harm me, but decades later, here I was, the shame plain to see in all those shoes in my closets—more than I want to admit here. In my head, I knew the shoes I had used when I was a boy had worn out because they were inexpensive and because I was a busy boy with three paper routes. But in my heart, back then and still, I felt I had done something wrong with the shoes.

When I realized that feeling, that belief, had stayed with me, I began to work on reducing the number of shoes taking up space in my heart. And tried to remember how significantly every spoken word can impact another.

I kept running. It was an amazing release for me. One day, a friend asked if I could meet with someone who wanted to know more about chi running.

I met with her to show her the running techniques. Mamie and I continued after the lesson with a deep conversation. We could not stop speaking about life.

And my world stopped for a moment, just long enough for my soulmate to hop on and start it turning again.

I told one of my staff that I'd met a life-changing person named Mamie.

"Don't scare her," they said. "Don't be telling her your Buddha stuff. Don't overwhelm her with all this inner-happiness and life-journey stuff, okay?"

"Buddha stuff," indeed. I began to realize just how much I'd evolved, and how burdenless and authentic a life mine had become.

Through Mamie, I gained two university-age bonus children with whom I developed a great mutual respect, and for whom I felt genuine fatherly love.

Meeting Mamie and knowing we were going to spend our lives together allowed me to feel loved and valued as I never had before. I learned to love myself more through her story and then through creating our story.

Chapter 39

Vision Therapy

THOUGH MOST OF US SEE, we fall short in observation. Vision is the sum of biologically organized science in the body. And it is the result of the influence of environment and culture.

An image is created through one hand holding another hand, or gripping a pen, or wielding a weapon, or waving goodbye. Our fingertips seek out letters on a keyboard to create mental pictures of new worlds by combining words that form new ideas. A drumbeat evokes a clear picture of bars and notes on a musical staff. A mouthful of juicy peach has colour. A mouth full of lies appears jagged and sharp. Intuition provides insights far faster than the eyes.

When I opened my eyes again, after Mamie, I became deeply interested in the results of vision therapy.

In matters of the complete visual process, all roads lead to the brain, which leads to the heart, which leads to the soul and begs the theory that it is all connected—that in every cell there are hands, eyes, a mouth, a nose, and ears.

After a trauma, an accident, or even overworking, therapy is prescribed to remedy certain parts of the body or mind. Specific movements, exercises, and devices are employed to repair, restore, and resolve body issues. Pioneers in the field of vision therapy say it is like physical therapy for the eyes—and their power source: the brain.

Vision therapy is intended only to be delivered through optometrists. It is an evidence-based, highly researched therapy that involves retraining learned aspects of vision. The brain can form and reorganize synaptic connections—it does this through learning and experience. This is called neuroplasticity. This ability to reform offers ways forward for those who have experienced trauma, suffered strokes, been physically injured, exhibited dyslexia, and more.

Children and adults alike can benefit from vision therapy that includes a progressive program of procedures customized to each patient, using therapeutic lenses, prisms, filters, occluders or patches, electronic targets, and balance boards.

When I saw what neurotherapy/vision therapy could do, and knowing that seeing is believing, I knew I had to be part of it. It was a way I could continue to respond in new and more impactful ways to the needs of people who needed just this kind of help.

Stelios, Areef, and I became involved with classes and training offered by an array of incredible individuals who shared with us their methods and breakthroughs so that we could provide this therapy as part of our own professional services.

My connections with the pioneers in the field of vision therapy increased. People kept arriving at the office with needs. Daily, my heart burst with gratitude to the combination of wonder and science, and my heart went out to each person who came in with their story, which usually included years of unresolved treatment.

Many of the improvements were nearly instantaneous. I began videotaping my consultations as proof of how this science works so quickly and beautifully.

I prepared for the rest of the adventure. Everything seemed to fall into place to allow me to work with vision therapy and have Mamie's daughter, Dr. Meagan Lum—recently graduated in optometry—to handle the optometry business, and her mother, my life-partner and life-love Mamie, to run the entire administration. I focused on delivering the vision therapy.

Everything continued to fall into place.

Chapter 40

Ayahuasca

Except *EVERYTHING* WAS NOT FALLING into place. Like my anxiety over the washroom issue. The cells that had wound around my bladder and urethra and the messages being sent to my brain had been interfering in my life for long enough. I felt like I'd tried everything to heal my bladder issue. If a urologist couldn't help me, then it was time for someone, something, much larger to be called in to help.

I also had a nagging feeling that I had some work to do around my memories of my grandfather. And with the promise I'd made to my father that I would write our story. I wanted to better understand our family's trauma. It's true I had kept my word that my mother would never again have to suffer indignities like she had at the market in Letung, and I had become a doctor based on the inspiration of the medic who'd treated me in Air Raya. Yet I had unfinished business. Unfinished within myself.

Areef suggested I go to an ayahuasca ceremony—he had been to one himself and found it to be safe and life-changing. I didn't have anything to lose and potentially everything to gain.

Ayahuasca is a kind of tea made from plants and other ingredients that produce naturally occurring hallucinations. It's been used in spiritual and religious ceremonies by ancient tribes in the Amazon and is still used by some religious communities in North and South America today. And I thought it might help me.

All through 2018, I would search for and find a healing ayahuasca ceremony, and then something would get in the way of confirming the booking: a staff issue at work requiring immediate attention or a computer glitch. It was ridiculous. Then, in April 2019, I found one in Costa Rica that looked promising. Within ten minutes the reservations were made and paid for.

April 2019.

Almost forty years to the day since my family had left Vietnam.

I wasn't sure what to expect from my ayahuasca ceremony. I had read about or heard from others that it could be everything from unexplainable to magical. Nothing could have prepared me for what happened after I drank the tea.

Shortly before my departure, a new patient came in for vision therapy to help with his concussion issues. Together we solved them. During his treatments, he told me he kept seeing, in his mind's eye, a random symbol. I kept a copy of the symbol he'd sketched out, but I wasn't sure why.

Onboard the plane, the film they were playing was *The Matrix*. Was it a coincidence that an altered-reality movie was playing hours before I was to experience an altered reality? I knew there was more to come that would grow my heart and soul.

I closed my eyes and pictured a flame deep within.

"Chào." The voice seemed familiar; the Vietnamese "hello" was perfectly pronounced. "Flip it down, the tray in the back of the seat in front of you."

I opened my eyes, but the passenger beside me was absorbed in their book. I closed my eyes again.

"The tray. It goes up and down," said the child's voice. "Flip it."

I opened my eyes, moved the little lever, and the tray dropped.

"Isn't it amazing?" the boy's voice said. "Flight attendants will serve you food and, if you did decide to drink something, they put it on this magic table." There was wonder in his words. Then there wasn't.

"You've visited the plane's washroom twice already, and you haven't drunk anything since yesterday afternoon."

I spoke to the boy inside me with in-my-head words. "I have tried to fix this. Specialists don't know what's wrong."

"I want to know more about that flame you were thinking about a minute ago. Is it like the fire inside a dragon?"

"You always come around when I'm sleepy," I said. "And alone."

"But you're not alone. I'm always with you," the boy inside me said.

When the plane landed, someone from the retreat met me and drove me to a resort that was luxurious but not in a commercial sense. The main part of the building was set up for comfort, with soft sofas and pleasing décor. There was something familiar about it all. I breathed it all in, and it struck me. The symbol my recent patient had drawn for me was everywhere: from printed paper to wall hangings. It turned out to be an illustration representing the replication of cells: growth. I felt everything was as it needed to be.

A person didn't have to go to any of the ayahuasca ceremonies; one was held each of the four nights. Or they could attend but not consume the medicine. We were guided but not pressured. Yoga classes, mud baths, colonics, and lectures were offered. Guests and participants came from all over the world. Sixty of us were served organic food prepared by caring chefs.

On the first day there, I did yoga, ate delicious food, and attended a talk about spirituality and life. Another session stressed the importance of nutrition and emphasized the need to drink lots of fluids—but I didn't dare, even though it was hot, because dehydrated was my chosen safe state.

When the sun set, the place took on a deeper spiritual feel, with the moon and the stars twinkling soft acceptance. It felt like there was no barrier between me and the night sky.

Mats that were more like mattresses were spread out across the massive space. They surrounded a central shrine area where items symbolizing peace, kindness, and spirituality were displayed.

There were gentle helpers—their soft movements and simple white clothing made them look like angels—guiding us to choose our mattresses. I chose mine and made myself comfortable. Drummers drummed, dancers danced, and the angels went from mattress to mattress checking on each of us.

The washrooms were clearly marked, located on the periphery of the room. Of course I checked them out. They were clean and modern.

Nothing about the event felt strange or uncomfortable. Each person was an individual with their own internal reasons, and yet we were gathered as one, our presence overlapping with those who were employed to provide service. It was like we were each our own island, yet a part of the whole.

I relaxed into it and listened to the instructions in the speech given by the founder of the resort. A shaman spoke about the medicine.

Choreographed, I thought. Beautifully so. And I didn't have to know the dance steps. I was confident ayahuasca would lead the way.

I felt as if I was on a river and the river itself. Like a clear, undiscovered river nestled in the most majestic mountains. There was peace. It was lovely. There was a sacred ritual feel to it all—and we hadn't even taken any medicine yet.

To prepare for the ayahuasca drink, we first had to inhale through the nose a mix that was a thousand times stronger than wasabi. It burned. It cleared my head, not that it needed clearing. Immediately after, I took the small glass and drank the mixture. It soothed the burning.

I felt no fear. I was open to anything and everything.

I let go and let guidance.

I let go and let spirit.

I was absorbed in the moment, and the next, and the next, and in each moment I, in turn, was absorbing it all.

The next thing I knew, I was writing on the mattress with my hand, no pen, just the idea of the book that had been a promise to my father. I remembered the notes I had packed away before moving house.

The angel people checked on me as I was feeling nauseous. And then—

Buddha arrived.

Not someone dressed as Buddha. Not like a Santa Claus at a company Christmas party, or how my roommate in university had dressed up as a mascot. Nor was it a hologram, like in the haunted house at Disneyland where images of ghosts are projected on the walls. Buddha just popped in. Right above me. In the form of a salamander. Yet I knew it was Buddha.

"What do you want, Vi Tu? Why are you here?" Buddha asked.

I blurted out my urinary problem. And the decades of needing a bathroom close by, of excessive peeing, of embarrassment about having to leave several times during presentations or in lineups. I told of withholding liquids from myself until I was dangerously dehydrated—all so that I could avoid peeing. I wanted to be cured. I wanted the problem to end.

I looked up at Buddha, and Buddha spoke to me inside my head. They were not words in any language I knew, and not like a download might work on a computer, not how some people say ideas arrive through energy. But Buddha spoke:

"You can get off the boat now, Boy. It is time."

I took a deep breath. The mattress underneath me confirmed I was in the big building at the event, with drummers drumming, dancers dancing, and angels checking on me.

I listened to those words as I had never listened to any words before and repeated them in my head:

"You can get off the boat now, Boy. It is time."

And then I *was* the child-me. And I was on the boat. The boat that crumbled into the sea. I saw all the passengers on 4581: the newborn and the aged, rows of people holding each other up even when they might be unconscious.

And there was nowhere to pee.

And Buddha said:

"You can do this. Get off the boat."

Get off the boat. But how?

Where were people peeing? Where were they defecating? The boat rocked from side to side. The scent of desperation hung in a cloud over our vessel, adrift in the South China Sea.

The tiny bathroom that was not adequate for one family, let alone hundreds of people. The vomit, the urine, the feces.

We had nowhere to urinate. Our dignity, stripped.

The boy in me began to weep, and I asked the boy inside me not to cry. I told the boy that our dignity had *not* been stripped from us, that our courage had to rise above any shame over being reduced to a struggle for basic needs. We had to do what we had to do so that we could live another hour, another day. Because that's what humans do. We could get over our trauma. We would get over our trauma.

The Buddha had called me Boy. The whole present-moment in Costa Rica was rocking under my mattress because I was on the South China Sea. The boat was crumbling.

I looked down at my shorts, and then to a daytime cloudless sky, and then to the 4581 written on the side of the boat, then behind me to an endless ocean. I turned my head to face forward with my body, then stepped carefully on rotting wooden planks and off the side of the boat into a space filled with light and, as I did, a gangplank appeared under my feet, then stretched to an unrecognizable pier.

"It is over," Buddha said.

In that moment, my brain hung up on what had been a lifetime call with my bladder. My bladder sighed, then replaced the phone in its cradle.

I knew the peeing problem was gone. Forever. And so was Buddha.

Eventually, I returned to my room and enjoyed a peaceful sleep. In the morning, fresh juices and clear water tasted like sunshine. I took a bottled beverage and stretched out in a hammock, which rocked gently in the breeze.

Over the next three nights, I once again participated in the ceremony. I had no more problems to solve, but I had conversations with Nelson Mandela and Dr. Wayne Dyer.

Each day, I'd wake rested, attend yoga, and delight in the taste of fresh mango juice, coconut water, and herbal iced tea. I noticed the glasses holding these beverages and realized I was more than a half-full person. I was a profoundly-grateful-for-the-vessel-itself person. Not once did I have anything other than a normally spaced interval between bathroom urges. My bladder functioned just as a human bladder should.

One afternoon, in the quiet of the day, only the breeze moving the fronds of the coconut palms, I closed my eyes and returned to Air Raya. All that manual labour: fetching water, cutting trees with a tiny knife. So many steps I must have walked through the tropical island paths. Not as many as my grandparents had taken, I'm sure, but enough to know that I had endured an epic adventure.

I remembered that at one time, back in Vietnam, I'd expected to go to Hong Kong with my grandfather, after the fall of Saigon. What kind of life would I have had then? How would I have come to know myself as I knew myself, in this moment, sitting in Costa Rica? I registered a crushing but passing wave of sadness as I thought about how my grandfather had stopped whispering to me, and how I had felt he had abandoned me. I saw that this wasn't the truth. My grandfather hadn't abandoned me; I had let go of him. I had to so that I could be me.

A glorious feeling washed over me. I was and would always be connected to my grandfather, and to every human and creature and plant. We all walk about in each other's footsteps, absorbing energy from those who walked before us, and generating energy for those who will walk after. All over the world.

A chessboard has sixty-four squares. A black safe can only hold so much treasure. A standard piece of paper can be folded upon itself a finite amount of times. But time folds over and over in an overlapping story that cannot be contained. Connectedness is undeniable, and it is necessary to forgive the self and others to sustain life and grow love.

I looked up at the sky, and held my bare feet to the ground, and the Earth shifted again.

When clocks became essential again and I went to the airport, I didn't feel the need to seek out every washroom. I boarded my flight without worrying whether my seat was close to the toilet.

"Chào, hola, hi." The boy in me spoke shortly after takeoff.

"Are you trying to impress me with your Vietnamese, Spanish, and English?" I asked.

"We were amazing, weren't we?"

"We are more than you and me," I said. "Everything and everyone are connected."

"Even salamanders and dragons?" asked the boy.

"My heart is full of love," I said.

"My heart is filled with fire," said the boy. "And a book."

I landed in Toronto and thought about symbolism, be it the one for cellular growth, a salamander, or a dragon. The boy had spoken to me on the plane much as my grandfather's wisdom used to, just as the house on the hill had. How could I pay more attention to life? The Chinese character for listening came to mind. I focused on its parts. And somewhere between Pearson airport welcoming me back and Uxbridge welcoming me home, I was closer to fulfilling the promise to my father, and nearer to changing one billion lives.

Chapter 41

Africa Speaks Again

Just as I was overcome in Africa, had placed my hand on my heart and opened my arms and said, "Here," I found myself doing the same thing after ayahuasca. This time, I stood in Uxbridge. This time, I had experienced profound healing and a deep connection. And this time, there was no question that here in the heart and here on the whole planet were the same place. I stretched myself to agree with the boy inside me and the grandfather who was part of me that awareness of the universe is enough to understand we are all one.

My thoughts became so deep that I began to crave silence to let the ideas and awareness rest. Meditation did that.

My twelve little wooden elephants were out in the world. They'd come forward in the gift shop and been restless in my pocket when I returned, and I'd given them out as soon as I got back to Canada.

Not long before, I'd said to Stelios and Areef that I wanted to change the world and influence one billion people. Some of it could be done, I thought, by sharing scientific breakthroughs relating to vision and the brain, and by revealing what I'd learned at an ayahuasca, where a serious personal problem of four decades had been eliminated in a matter of minutes. I also thought millions could be affected by spreading the word in a tell-twelve-friends-they-tell-twelve-friends way, relaying the peace-inducing, simple lessons of the masters—knowledge that encourages true consciousness.

Once I'd handed out the little elephants to their perfect matches, I'd become further immersed in service to help those with concussion injuries and sight-related issues. I brought myself to the feet of the lessons of my grandfather, and all the grandfathers before him, all the way back to the masters who floated the concepts of virtues and touted the validity of karma. Waves of forgiveness washed over me and continued to be a steady companion to me if I started to become frustrated with someone.

Even though I had given the elephants to twelve people, they were out there for everyone in the world because of my intention to positively influence one billion people, twelve at a time, so that they could pay forward the freedom and joy that comes with gratitude. The pages of the book that I'd once seen floating away from the wake of a boat on the South China Sea were becoming a reality. They would represent elephants too. I pictured every reader finding beauty in themselves and beginning to feel a connection to others by recognizing their self-worth through resilience, patience, perseverance, passion and purpose, communication, creativity and trust, intuition, benevolence, confidence, integrity, curiosity, and forgiveness. Every reader could become an ambassador of gratitude and, through that thankfulness, find themselves and therefore discover inner peace.

Africa spoke again and again, through symbols.

Just as elephants carry seedlings in their big feet and contribute to the planet by increasing plant and tree diversity, so do we carry seeds inside our heart that are spread through acts of kindness and benevolence as well as by opening our arms to others and by being of service.

When we perform even the smallest of actions or graciously receive kindness from someone else, we all become safer. Like when the communities in Africa acted to protect the elephants from poachers, and the people felt safer and could take their shoes off at night and sleep barefoot for the first time.

And to extend it would be to share that just as the poachers were perceived as evil in their acts toward the community and the elephants, so do we face evil in our own communities. What is required as a deeper dip into the well of goodness is to work out how to create connection so that we can begin to understand and work toward forgiveness of what we term as evil or bad. And we can keep working at that with connection so that generations coming behind us can evolve into peacemakers.

We change the world one step at a time, beginning with our own.

And we remind ourselves that our own world is our body, mind, and soul, and these are part of a larger wonder. Then we take another step. And another. And we continue to be part of that folding over of a timeline.

I kept taking steps. Another few years had passed. People were coming from far and wide for vision therapy. I was pleased with the results. I was changing lives.

Chapter 42

Dragons, Fathers, and Green Tea

Enter 2024, the Year of the Dragon. My life was full and, while beautiful, more hectic than I desired. I was second-guessing my spiritual role, again—feeling as if there was something still in the way of my being at true peace. Besides, the more I saw success from vision therapy work, the more I wanted to delve into the workings of humanness and connection with spirit and energy.

I decided to attend a Vipassana retreat. The teachings were based on Buddha's wisdom; Areef (Gandhi) and Stelios (Aristotle) had each attended. I, who they had always called Buddha, was not about to be left behind.

It would involve spending ten days in silence. Ten days! The concept terrified me; could I even go a single day without speaking? And how would I avoid making eye contact with other attendees? There was to be no reading or writing, no formal exercise, no stimulants. Ten days of silence, except for a one-hour lecture each evening. A simple vegetarian menu would be provided.

How would I manage with nothing to do? The rules would be difficult for those of us who are attached to our phones, are active on social media, run businesses, and are used to freely chatting with those in our lives. I knew it would be one of the hardest things I'd ever do. Yet I knew I had to go.

The venue was not far from Uxbridge. Mamie drove me there, in part because if I didn't have a car, I would have no escape. I'd heard that some people make it only a few days before they decide to leave. I didn't want to give myself that out.

On the first day, I went through the motions, conscious of the looming third day when most people quit. At the first lecture, I heard that the body is made up of water, air, earth, and fire. But when I sat with myself, all I saw was earth and fire. My insides were an apocalyptic site of scorched territory: from my trauma of the decades-ago escape from Vietnam, the frantic pace of life, and the diet I had been consuming. I could understand that the inside me lacked water and air, because all I saw was smoke. But I had no idea how to change that.

I began to grasp the concept of equanimity, which is a calmness or evenness of the mind even when in difficult situations. When we have strong responses to something, we are not experiencing equanimity. Let's say you are running low on your favourite breakfast granola, but before you can replenish it, you learn the brand is no longer available. You become sad or obsessed with what it will be like when you cannot have it anymore. Then it becomes available again, and you're excited, running to the store on your lunch break to stock up. In both cases, this is a loss of balance, an unbalanced response to the granola. Equanimity means to simply enjoy the breakfast that is there in the moment and to not be concerned about it when you are not eating it.

Even though I was focusing on goodness and kindness and giving back, I came to see that my own thoughts were out of balance. I needed equanimity around food. I knew that I didn't want to experience the unpleasantness of not having something I wanted. I needed a balanced mind without craving.

I needed a better inner landscape. I knew I needed to handle the scorching fire inside me.

On the third day, the teacher called on me. When I received the request to see him, I felt like I'd been called to the principal's office.

"I've seen this resistance in others in this program over many years," he said to me. "Most times, I just let them go, I let them leave after the third day."

I squirmed in my seat.

"But you, Vi Tu, you have to do the hard work." He told me that he felt compelled to intervene in my case because he knew I had to do this. And that I could.

After three days, and three lectures, and a visit to the principal's office, I discovered I could sit, lotus position with no cushion, for one whole hour without moving. I could go all day without making eye contact or speaking. When the 4 a.m. gong sounded on the fourth day, it was like waking in a sacred sound bath.

I started to take just green tea throughout the day and an apple at night. That was all my body seemed to need. The smoke inside me began to dissipate. My body calmed. I felt more balanced.

Still, I was agitated in other ways.

The next several days unfolded. Still, just green tea all day and an apple at night. Less agitation. Deeper meditation.

On the seventh day, the predawn gong went off. I emerged from sleep to the appearance of spheres behind my still-closed eyes—dozens of spheres. Was this a sign of entering stages of enlightenment I'd heard about? Could I be becoming enlightened? Was I in an altered state? My body was a garden. No smoke or fire anywhere.

As I opened my eyes, *whoosh.*

A dragon appeared right in front of my face.

"Hello, Vi Tu," he said. "This is your father speaking."

But the voice was not my father in Toronto. It was my uncle who had passed away before my birth, the one who had come through an oracle when my mother was sick during her pregnancy, who made the deal that she would be fine if she committed to giving me over to my grandfather as a substitute for him. I *had* always thought of him as another father, a sort of spiritual father.

"I'm here to tell you that this is the year to release your book." He was referring to a family member's anxiety around my book, this book. He said this person had their own issues, agenda, trauma, and pain. But it was not my pain, he explained.

"I'm so proud of you," the dragon said.

The dragon was my uncle, my grandfather, my father (who was still alive in Toronto), and the boy inside me. It was all the power and drive within me that I had been gifted from all those in my past—a lineage of courage and strength. The dragon, in all its glorious colour, whooshed out again between the spheres.

I finished the final days of the Vipassana. Ideas downloaded during my meditations. I began to see that when you are chaos, you get chaos. I could see myself and my behaviour as a set of mirrors that created time-crunch issues for me.

At the final mealtime, I broke down and began to sob. I could not stop crying. Actually, I did not try to stop. All I could do was experience it and let the beast rise and fall. I saw the image of my brother holding his son, the one who had passed away as a child. My brother's pain flooded through me. I felt his anger and his fear of losing control. My tears continued.

As my heart calmed and the sorrow levelled, I was invited once again to go and speak to our teacher.

"These feelings of and for others happen here, Vi Tu," he said. "You can let it go now. You do not have to fight the battles of others, for others." He told me to simply observe, to balance, to trust that I would find myself in a state of equanimity.

At the final lecture that night, I listened to two stories that were simple and powerful. The first one was a story of a professor and a fisherman who was providing the academic a ride in his boat to an island.

In his arrogance—and need to feed his ego—the professor asked the fisherman if he knew about oceanography.

"I have no formal education, sir," the fisherman replied.

The professor told the fisherman how sad he was for him and mentioned how much of the man's life was wasted by not formally studying the oceans, and that there were so many aspects to water that were essential to know.

"Have you been schooled in meteorology, to understand the weather and to identify storms and types of clouds?" the professor asked the fisherman.

"I just take care of the basics," said the fisherman. "And I appreciate the power and beauty of my surroundings."

The professor explained how sad this was, that the uneducated were ignorant and wasteful of their lives. "What about navigation, sonar, radar, and the latest in scientific findings and GPS technology?" asked the professor.

But the fisherman had much the same answer, and patiently smiled when the professor told the fisherman he'd wasted so much of his life.

For the rest of the day, the professor regaled the fisherman with the awards and accolades he'd received in academia.

Grey clouds appeared overhead, and it started to rain.

"Professor," said the fisherman, "do you know anything about swimming?"

"Why would I need to know that?" asked the professor. "I was busy studying the water, not playing in it."

"I feel sad for you," said the fisherman. "There's a pretty good chance this boat is going for a wreck."

This story about a boat and the sea brought forth images of 4581 and 4518, along with the thousands of people who had given their lives to the South China Sea, and the thousands that had populated those remote islands. *Was this story for me?* It seemed an odd coincidence. But perhaps there are no coincidences.

The next story made me more certain than ever that there are no coincidences, for it was a story about none other than an elephant.

The story began with three individuals who had been born without eyesight. Now, as adults, they were brought before an elephant.

The first individual was at the front of the elephant. "Interesting," said the person. "I can feel a long column that curls on itself. An elephant must be a hose."

The second person was at the back of the elephant. "Wow," said the person. "There is a brushlike quality. It's softer than paintbrush bristles. An elephant must be made of feathers."

The third person was beside the elephant's leg. The individual brought their arms around the thick leg and focused on the texture and size. "Wow," said the individual. "An elephant must be a tree trunk."

Each of them had told the truth. Their own truth. A partial truth. Whether it served them in the future would be based on their sharing and their willingness to listen to each other.

In the final moments of the Vipassana retreat, I took back the rules that there was to be no writing, and, within half an hour, I wrote ten pages of download that was an upgrade of my life: how to better run the office, how to spend better time with Mamie, how to find a new peace. It was a massive and powerful set of guidelines that I began to put into practice immediately.

I returned home in time to make this final addition to the book. But as I spoke to my editor and publisher, I was reminded that the book will never be finished, because it is part of an ambassadorship, a part of a tell-two-friends, a part of a larger activity of listening to each other.

Epilogue

My parents remain in the house across from Humber College that Ted found and Doris's loan for the down payment funded. The campus has grown around them. I've tried to talk them into moving, as others have, but they do not listen. It is their home. Chinatown is not far. They know the buses. They are familiar with the community. They have over forty years of memories in the little house that once held more than a dozen family members. The big pot of rice is still a feature of the kitchen.

At the time of writing, Barbara is ninety-seven years old, and I remain in contact with her, helping in any way I can—duties that could never repay her for all that she did.

Cory, the huge fluffy mascot who studied biology, became a teacher. It is the perfect path for him—every learner needs a cheerleader. His students' lives are improved because he is teaching the kind of fun he used to teach me. We are still in touch.

Dr. Meagan Lum and I continue to sponsor the Ted Murphy Awards.

Mrs. Fowles, who had been there when I was a new Canadian, arrived at my office not that long ago, now in her eighties, overwhelmed when I explained that returning to Uxbridge and setting up my practice there was about being able to give back, to continue the legacy of all those who had been such a help to me and my family. Following my reunion with Mrs. Fowles, she wrote me an incredible letter about karma, the organic flow of giving, and all the goodness that comes from that. Not long after her appointment, one of her children, a son who became a lawyer, took a running class I facilitated. We reminisced about all those years ago and the values his parents held and taught.

There are good people in this world, and by "good" I mean filled with goodness and connected to the innocence and nonjudgemental ways that they were born with. The twelve sponsors and all those connected to sponsoring my family and all the families are examples. They are the twelve elephant ambassadors who each have a little wooden elephant in their pocket, that they might roll out some of their hardness and leave it on a mountain, that they might remember their own struggles and then find a way to incite positive change in an area of their life they thought impossible.

I am proof that anything is possible. My chess-brain is also now a soft thinking place. Strategy and love are meant to go together.

What has emerged so far for me in this journey is that we learn from each other so we can understand our self-worth through resilience, patience, perseverance, passion and purpose, communication, creativity and trust, intuition, benevolence, confidence, integrity, curiosity, and forgiveness. Twelve behemoth subjects. Twelve elephants. And we learn that we learn those subjects better when we are in a cooperative collective that is wrapped in a blanket of gratitude.

That's what it's all about, I have decided. Journeying to a place of thankfulness through the willingness to be thankful.

Just as me and my family were a part of more than a million people who had risked their lives by fleeing oppression, there were great numbers of people who took a massive chance and trusted that their benevolence toward refugees would not only be a decision of kindness but would benefit their communities.

Canada holds a good portion of those kind people.

Which brings me to more good people.

When I was a child on Air Raya, I didn't know that decisions were being made for Canada to organize how they would receive refugee families. I had no idea Canadian Forces Base Griesbach, in the city of Edmonton, was actively housing military families at that time and that those families and the staff on base were advised that they would be the receiving point to process all Vietnamese refugees who had been accepted by Canada.

While my family was on one side of the world, clinging to hope that the Canadian family that had stepped forward to sponsor us would not change their mind, other refugees had arrived in Canada and were being welcomed by good people, given residency, and moved to various cities where sponsors were fully prepared.

When I first saw the military base in Edmonton, I was in awe, perhaps shock, having just flown around the world and into a climate so cold I could never have imagined it. It was only later, when I prepared to share my story, that I learned the reception centre at the Edmonton garrison eventually became the staging area for 25,000 refugees who arrived 500 at a time. At the busiest of times, those military families who lived on the base doubled and tripled up to make space in their homes for new arrivals.

The Edmonton base had been frantically organizing to accept refugees, each one taking about sixty man-hours to process through immigration and medicals. Even with small numbers of refugees arriving, the logistics were challenging. But those later groups of 500 at a time every six days caused massive changes in how the base operated.

Initially, people had to be hired to cook. Decisions had to be made as to what to feed all the newcomers. None of this would have been possible without the partnership of the people of Canada and various government levels. Faith communities, municipalities, not-for-profit agencies, and private individuals answered the global call for help. Canadian immigration officials cooperated in a massive project that would become the template for future refugee movements.

All those people had goodness in their hearts.

Still, there were things that could change, and did. Good people changed some of those things.

Here's one example of such a misstep and the correction of a policy.

None of us had appropriate clothing for the climate—no one had much of anything at all. Refugees arrived in Edmonton in clothing they had been wearing since leaving the camp, and sometimes they'd been wearing the same thing for days or even weeks before that. Undergarments were to be surrendered and incinerated, and they'd get a full set of fresh clothes.

One evening, there was a disturbance in the Edmonton barracks when a Vietnamese woman became distraught. An interpreter was summoned and drove across Edmonton in the middle of the night, and the public relations person facilitated the frantic conversation.

In the excitement of arriving in Canada and then being asked to discard her underwear in exchange for new ones, she had momentarily forgotten that her bra contained her future. A year earlier, when the family had sold all their possessions, they had purchased a diamond, which was then sewn into her bra.

A massive dumpster filled with underwear and other things slated for incineration was searched. After a detailed and unpleasant sifting, the bra was found, the diamond recovered, and it was returned to the family.

This was a uniquely respectful and Canadian response to one person's distress. I sometimes wish I could be face-to-face with those responders and thank them from the bottom of my heart for the respect they gave the situation and the woman, and for their honesty.

The policy was changed thereafter, but not without a bit of a fuss and a lot of debate. An official working directly with the refugees said to immigration policymakers that if the underwear-surrendering policy were to continue without alteration, they would ship every piece of underwear to the official's office—boxes worth. It worked. It was decided that, should any refugee wish to keep their underwear, they could wash them in machines provided. Many didn't want to keep their old underwear, but it was a step in allowing people to retain some dignity and to be offered choice.

Oh, Canada, I often say in my mind. *I love you.* If only every situation like that was resolved by stopping, listening, feeling for the person, and then acting with respect.

There are good people everywhere. Good is a subjective term.

Every person I met at the Bến Thành marketplace, whether they were buyers or other vendors, whether they were American or Vietnamese, offered a mirror for me to see myself. Each person I met on Air Raya, Letung, and Galang, whether they had fled Vietnam or were part of the UN personnel, showed to me a part of myself by revealing a part of themselves. The officials guarding the Malaysian refugee camp who pointed weapons on us allowed me to see the story of their life and write my own. From the person who put the blue toque on my head to the lady who purchased a pair of shoes for me that were two dollars—each of them demonstrated their values and held them up to me, which allowed me to examine, evaluate, and grow mine. Dr. Tam's decision to take me into that storage room and show me the box of valium demonstrated his values and helped me activate mine. Dr. Tam could have simply written a prescription. The soldiers could have fired their weapons and killed us. The lady could have chosen not to buy me shoes, bought me expensive ones, or replaced the ones that I wore holes into. The choices we make are wholly connected to our value system.

We are all mirrors, and mirrors reflect. When I meet you, I am a mirror for you to look at yourself. You can see yourself and hear yourself through the refraction of light that I provide. You are not really looking at me; you are looking into yourself.

Each of us is both a map of life and a compass. Our service to others, our compassion, our empathy, our aggression, and our judgement are generated not by what we see but how we interpret what we see in relation to ourselves.

ORACLES AND DRAGONS

Oracles and fortune tellers are part of our Vietnamese culture. But it was not until this manuscript went to the publisher that I discovered my father had seen more than one.

In 2023, my father confided in me that before we left Vietnam, he'd seen an oracle who told him that we must escape. The oracle said not only that we would leave on a boat, but also which boat we would be on. Another oracle assured my father that he and the family would survive the escape attempt, because he was born in the Year of the

Dragon, and there would be two boats involved in his escape and they were both dragons too.

Three dragons? Told to my father before I'd even conceived of the promise for this book?

When I began this book, I engaged in the first meeting with Marie. The morning after the interview, she called me and explained she did not usually do what she had done, but her vision after the call had been so powerful that she had to write it out—and would I read it?

What Marie wrote was the scene of the boy, and the man, *and the dragon*. At that time, neither of us had any idea about the oracles' words involving dragons to my father.

In all the years we've been preparing this book, pushing and pulling and revising, that piece of writing has barely changed and has remained at the beginning of every draft. Fifty years after an oracle spoke to my father about his being a dragon and two boats being dragons, someone I'd met for but an hour had a vision of a dragon inside me and expressed the courage of my father and tied it to a promise I'd made him.

I am no longer surprised.

THE COURAGE INSIDE YOU

Once upon a true time, there was an extraordinary story that contained temples, an old boat on a treacherous ocean, tropical islands, and treasure. In the backdrop were weapons, war, and heartbreaking goodbyes. Its narrative was carried by resilience and enduring spirit.

"I've heard this, already," you say.
"This is the ending," says the boy. "And you're in it."

The story kept mostly to itself until, one day, Past bumped into Future in a hallway of an ordinary house in Ontario, Canada, and discovered a story. After Past and Future had steadied themselves, they got to chatting about what they'd found: a boy and a man in the same person.

It didn't take long to put their observations together and align in their wish that the story should not remain in the house, nor in the heart of a child inside a man; they knew it was powerful enough to change the lives of individuals who heard the story. So, they conspired to outline how the story could be told so that it did exactly what they wanted it to, which was to inspire people, to help them grow, to ease their suffering, to bring them hope and love.

When Past and Future had finished, they knew they would need to summon a dragon to help them find their cohort, Present, in the demanding work of writing a book.

The dragon was not easily woken, but when it was, it only took moments to locate Present. But it took a long time for Present to creatively put down the story—there were stops and starts, mostly because of Past's trauma, and Future's cousin, Fear. When Present picked up the pen, Opportunity appeared. So did Fear.

Past, Present, and Future rejoiced. Dragon exhaled fire and burned away Fear. All that was left was for Opportunity to head out into the world and show up at the front doors of people—as if opportunity was a travelling salesperson, but with a more interesting product than Fuller brushes or encyclopedias.

Opportunity is in your hands now. You can welcome it as a long-lost friend. You are an elephant ambassador now if you choose to be.

You may be an elephant ambassador, but there's a dragon inside you too.

The Twelve Elephant Ambassadors

In the wild, elephants stand in groups called herds. When they journey—even the shortest trips—they are referred to as a parade. And what is a parade? It's a moving forward with others, in the same direction, for the purpose of celebration. This feels like what I was doing each time I joined like-minded people in my Canadian world who were involved in acts of service and kindness.

JUDY

One of the twelve people I knew must have an elephant is Judy Machado. I've always called her an angel. She is a river of love. She has said that her hands tingled when I placed the elephant into them. "Everything from you is a high-frequency message and a guide for my soul," she said. Then she told me she was eager to participate in a love story of life.

Judy Machado naturally sees the light in all, even when it is dark—especially when it is dark. She helps people see the light within themselves, and she uses the alchemy of love and plant medicine to do that (cacao). I knew that she would help people invite new perspectives into their lives so that they can be taken beyond conditioned and limited beliefs. I have always believed in her mission, passion, and purpose, which is always the expression of love to support awakening. What I didn't know when I gave Judy her elephant is that she'd be the one to introduce me to my scribe, my collaborator who has helped me create this book.

AREEF

Areef has the kind of effect on people that shows them that they are on their own journey of discovery. He's so wise, I began to call him Gandhi. He said that when I placed the elephant in his hand, he became flooded with loving responsibility.

"Over time, it has become a motivator, encouraging me— even on low days—to change the world, reminding me the smallest gesture of kindness does just that," he said.

Areef invites people to see the big picture, to think about all the roles they would want as well as those they don't want. He reminds us to always listen, learn, and love; to trust that the answers are within; and to find the joy in watching others succeed because that kind of witnessing builds character and grows one's own success.

NANCY

Nancy is the kind of person who appears when the sun's rays bounce off stained-glass windows to play colourful games across your face.

I gave Nancy an elephant at a conference. I invited her to join me on an improvised stage, then presented her with the carving. She has said that the little wooden creature immediately became a part of her life and that it reminded her that we were all gentle giants, carefully treading sacred ground, walking home with each other, a steadily growing parade of humans on a road called Life.

Nancy is both a window and a window opener. She helps people thrive by holding space for others to imagine life from a different vantage. She shows people how to let the sun and moon shine through them. She makes me think that when you are the light, you are the love.

BRANDON

Brandon is one of my soulmate's two children. I gave Brandon the elephant when he was in his second year of dental school. He knew about them, and knew there were twelve, and that I had already given some away. He understood that it wasn't simply passing something along—that the gesture was bigger.

Brandon saw his elephant as a responsibility for him to extend his interactions with others to promote their success.

"I knew I needed to grow into its meaning," he told me later. "I placed it in my room on my bookshelf at eye level.

Every time I sat or lay down, there it would be, right there for me to ponder its meaning. Then I realized that 'contemplating meaning' is a thing in itself. That the act of thinking about action and impact is a meaningful part of any plan."

Brandon invites and encourages people to think about their future at their own speed and learn from the success of others.

STELIOS

"Courage is the first of human qualities because it is the quality which guarantees the others." These are the famous words of Aristotle of Stagiritis from more than 2,000 years ago. They can also be attributed to my friend Stelios, whose name is short for Aristotle. He is completely into growth and courage. He reminds people how the scary things are always supported—even when we don't think they are. He loves helping others see how courageous they can be. Stelios has a bold presence, and that allows him to take his gifts and show others how sharing our gifts creates positive community. His commitment to improving lives by getting people to step into help is summed up poetically:

Rise.
laugh
until you cry.
move
out of your own way.
breathe in
your own magic.

make
your own dreams come true.
do this by
serving others and
living from love
because
only by taking your own vision of a situation to a great
　　height will you gain perspective.

CORALEE

The world is a safe place when you know someone has your back. Coralee is one of those someones. I knew she would be a perfect ambassador. Her elephant basically jumped out of my pocket and into her hands. Here's how she talks about its arrival.

"Once upon a time, I was at a dinner party with a group of friends in Toronto, Canada. There was laughter and lots of chatter, and people were circulating, as they do, visiting in little groups. One moment I was laughing at someone's silly story, and the next I had taken myself away from the group. Suddenly, there was a small, carved elephant in my hand. So delicate were its features that I became mesmerized. When I looked to see who had gifted it, I saw Vi Tu. His gentle speech laid out my task. He saw me as a game-changer in the world. I was both flabbergasted and humbled. The elephant and its symbol became a part of me instantly. It gave me a feeling of belonging to something bigger than myself. I felt a call to action, of responsibility to a higher cause. I believe he saw we had a shared vision: a better world."

Coralee believes we create a better world when we are sincere—when we have a genuine interest in what others are doing and why they are doing it. She believes that we all flourish through that connection. She believes that when we dedicate ourselves to love, we will uncover the higher potential of others, and our own.

KIRAN

I love the way Kiran tells the story of what she thought when she met me and how she owns it and talks about the lessons in it.

"A few years back, at a meeting, one of the attendees named Vi Tu was noticeably silent until the end of the session. Then he spoke, explaining that if we wish fear to leave, then we need to be calm; after that, everything we want will come to us. He asked us all to meditate.

"I remember asking, lightheartedly, 'Who invited the quack?'

"Despite the humorous intention, I judged. I had no idea I'd met a visionary at that time.

"The following year we were taking courses together, a group of us, Vi Tu included. Because of logistics, he picked me up to drive me to the course. From the outset, it felt like we knew each other. When we pulled over at a gas station, he gave me the elephant and described his vision of reaching one billion people through goodness. That little wooden animal immediately filled me with energy and ambition. The elephant is with me every day—and symbolizes the change that I made, and the change I can support in others."

Kiran's advice about meeting others is to give love to everyone you meet and do it by focusing on one thing you like about them, then delivering an authentic compliment—that is a sure way to avoid being judgemental.

MEAGAN

Meagan is my soulmate's daughter. She has pursued optometry; we work together. Beyond that, Meagan has infinite creativity. She saw her elephant as an extension of imagination.

Meagan understands that while age and experience are important, that does not mean that the inexperienced are not contributors. She understands that, and participation shapes those changes. As one who views life as art—and thrives on visual narratives in display, colour, style, and even trend—she believes optimism is vital to life. Meagan advises to always look for the goodness in people and situations; kindness and caring can be expressed in many ways, including gentleness and thoughtfulness around those who are experiencing difficulties; laughter and lightheartedness; and above all, listening. Compassionate listening is the key to creating community.

BOB

Bob Sanet is a pioneer in the science of vision and the brain. He opened the door for me to further my purpose. Though he has influenced many, his has directly created careers that have led to doctors healing tens of thousands. He has said his calling was expanded when he received the elephant from me. I know that he's the kind of person—a door

opener—who leads people to places where they learn gratitude, kindness, respecting differences, speaking from the
heart, and encouraging others. He tells people they have a
superpower and, if they don't know what it is, to go through
as many doors as they need to find it. He is one of the
humblest people I know.

KATHY

Kathy and I attended high school together. I sent her pictures
of Africa when I was there and knew that she would have to
have an elephant because she is part of a larger change in the
world. Kathy believes that no one is above or below anyone
else. Her ways include compassion and empathy, kindness,
and adventure. She advises people to truly live rather than
merely exist or survive, to see each day as a gift, and to seek
out new experiences within that gift. She asks people to listen
to their heart and to discover the beauty of leaning into
vulnerability. I was honoured to help Kathy find her calling
and knew that she would go on to help many others. Kathy
encourages me to feel the freedom that comes from opening
ourselves to the world.

FABIAN

Fabian is about strength. He encourages people to step into
new versions of themselves. He says that's what he did when
he was gifted one of the twelve elephants.

He is a believer in connection. He says we do not know
the potential that our actions hold—even the smallest. Or

especially the smallest. One tiny shift in behaviour, one miniscule stretch of a smile, one moment of decision to wave someone through, or even just wave, can be life changing. His wisdom includes encouraging people to be open-minded, to hear all sides of the story told during challenging times, and to be present for family and friends and for the self.

He taught me to see beginnings as gifts rather than burdens, as opportunities to be myself, fully and unapologetically.

MAMIE

Mamie is my soulmate, my noon and my midnight and every minute between. She has a great presence in the lives of others. She is also an ambassador of goodness.

"When I was active in corporate life, I learned to run to reduce stress—that was my solution. I had no knowledge of little, wooden elephants that were created to change the world. I wasn't even sure my world needed to be changed. I'd experienced joys and heartbreaking events along my way. I was, I believed, a typical businessperson living in a big city with an excess of responsibilities.

"The individual I met was more than a running coach. He was a pacing coach. A life-pacing, embrace-the-spaces teacher from Uxbridge. He believed our dreams were a part of our reality. When he presented me with the elephant, I knew the game-changing had been kicked into high gear.

"I believe that we connect with others in many ways, two of which are: we see in them what we see in ourselves; and the opposite, we see in others what we'd like to see in ourselves. Through that connection, we complete each other."

Mamie's influence is based on the values of unconditional love; a focus on the positive; gratitude; and embracing simplicity by focusing on one step at a time, whether it is studying a flower petal by petal or enjoying a meal by experiencing each mouthful.

THE MATH FOR ONE BILLION

Begin with presenting twelve people with a little wooden elephant, and ask them to influence twelve other people, and to ask those people to consciously work to influence twelve more.

Those people influence twelve people in their sphere.

144 people.

144 people each affect twelve people.

1,728 people

1,728 people each impact twelve people.

20,736 people

20,736 people each boost the thoughts of twelve people.

248,832 people

248,832 people bring joy to twelve people's lives.

2,985,984 people

2,985,984 people speak out to twelve people.

35,831,808 people

35,831,808 people are each kind to, and influence, twelve people.

429,981,696 more people are influenced.

If they each find twelve other people who they can offer a smile to, the number exceeds five billion.

Change the world. Heal the world. Grow the world.

Remembering

FOREVER IN MY HEART:

Ted Murphy (George Edward). Passed away February 15, 2008.

A father figure, chauffeur to soccer games, finder of our home, my golf teacher, my summer boss, later my accountant—always my friend.

"Call him Vi Ted," he said at the hospital when my brother Michael was born on Ted's birthday.

"You can't stay here," he said as he rallied to get us out of subsidized housing.

"You are family," spoken, implied, and demonstrated every day of his life.

~~~~~

Lloyd (Joseph Samuel) Ball. Passed away Saturday, July 27, 2013.

A man whose conversations were so deep they required few words.

A teacher by vocation and calling.

A fisherman who brought silence to water, introduced me to the lake, and quenched my thirst for connection.

~~~~~

Mary Beatrice Ball. Passed away Wednesday, December 24, 2014.

A constant servant, with community always at the forefront.

Mother, teacher, friend, mentor.

~~~~~

Doris Muckle. Passed away Tuesday, January 3, 2017.

A nurse by profession, she cared for all. She was the aunt every child wishes for. The host of sleepovers, the driver to summer jobs. The sit-at-the-table-and-eat-up nurturer. The confidante. The fixer. The soft place to fall.

"Read biographies. That is how you learn," she told me.

"Quick, get in the car and out of the cold," she said many times while driving me on my paper routes in the winter.

"You work so hard. Rest now," she said after collecting me and my siblings from strawberry picking.

"Good night, sleep tight, son," she'd say after a long day of seasonal work when I was a guest at her home.

Acknowledgements

I COULD NOT HAVE STARTED or completed this book without the selfless individuals who included me in their living stories.

MAMIE
you complete me,
you combine partnership, friend, and soulmate
and bring it to a love-and-trust-level
that I wish everyone could experience
. . . and then you go further, with the addition of
Brandon and Meagan,
whose integrity and talents will continue
a legacy of service.
The three of you fill me with pride,
joy, and laughter.

Linda Tse

You are a connector. Without you, I would
not have met Mamie.

My Parents

Your courage to recognize freedom as a necessity,
then take valiant action in the face of danger so
that your children could experience that liberty,
was a truly heroic journey.

My Siblings

With the deepest respect for your privacy
—you have your own stories—
I hold you in my heart as I share mine.

The Families Who Chose Us

Sponsors and citizens of Uxbridge, you knew
the human family knows no borders.
Gratitude abounds to **Michael McLuhan**
for initiating the sponsorship
and rescue-the-boat-people
movement in Uxbridge.

Barb and Ted Murphy—Lloyd and Mary Ball—Doris Muckle

You were my grandparents in every way, and
you redefined unconditional love and excelled in
benevolence, support, and guidance.

Lorne and Margaret Wall

You lifted us all on your shoulders, stepping in when childcare was needed, taking care of all of us while my mom brought a new life into the world.

John and Carole Fowles

You welcomed us into your home and showed us the Canadian way of life.

Nelson Cheung and John Wilson

Kindness, benevolence, trust, goodness

~~~

And to dozens of kind souls who showed kindness in so many ways that those ways themselves could be an instruction book of how to love

The Family We Chose

"Always love your friends from your heart and not from your needs."

—Buddha

Areef

"With every true friendship, we build more firmly the foundations on which the peace of the whole world rests."

—Mahatma Gandhi

Stelios

"Perfect friendship is the friendship
of men who are good,
and alike in excellence; for these wish well
alike to each other qua (who are) good,
and they are good in themselves."

—Aristotle

David Apps

My third chosen brother. Our relationship spans
decades and we've added a level of spirituality to our
golf games. David's kindness and wisdom are the
walls of a safe house where I can go and sit for awhile

To Colleagues, Mentors, and Teachers

Optometry. Dr. Sameen Chatoo

You were instrumental in helping me get into optometry school, writing my character reference letter,
offering guidance and support, coaching me about
my admission interview, and later in the practice of
optometry—such dedication of your time and
patience for which I am forever indebted.

Vision Therapy

I see you, and thank you, many times
a day in vignettes that play out in real time
with real people.

Drs. Nancy Torgerson, Trish Fink, Rob Lewis,
Bob Hohendorf, Bob Sanet, Cameron McCrodan,
Angela Peddle, Stefan Collier, Stel Nikolokakis,
Areef Nurani, Kiran Ramesh, Coralee Mueller,
Fabian Tai, Kara Peterson, Tanya Lewis Polec,
Paul Harris, and Caroline Hurst—you radiate
unconditional love and support
in helping me help others in this field.

The people of Uxbridge

Your trust in my practice means the world to me.

The infinite energetic family

To the twelve ambassadors of change who hold
simple carvings of elephants, our connection
is in perfect divine order, and my appreciation
is a deep river of love.
Areef, Bob, Brandon, Coralee, Fabian, Judy, Kathy,
Kiran, Mamie, Meagan, Nancy, Stelios

Danny

A dragon as old as time itself, you are the ultimate
guide to the universe. I'll not forget the day you
showed up at my office, without an appointment,
and said, "Your soul is starving." You showed
me what it meant to transcend guilt, shame, and
regret—how to live in harmony with nature
and the universe.

Yih Ling

We grew into adults and learned about life
and travel: Thank you for sharing the part of the
journey where we saw much of the world.

Thank you to the Dream Team

Judy: You knew who I should meet, and that
restarted it all. Your energy and knowingness
will forever be remembered.
Boni, John, and the entire Ingenium Books team:
passionate publisher extraordinaire, with combined
talents that confidently and graciously take
this creation into the world of readers; deeply
grateful am I for all the skills and dedication
you bring to a project.
Richard: an analyst, a scientist, a historian,
and an all-around sounding board behind
the scenes; this book is blessed with the
results of your integrity.

Marie

The translation of my heart language to written
word can only be explained (as we have both
decided, as we've pondered for hours) as this:
In another lifetime, in the Far East, there was a
gifted scribe who was dedicated to a wise elder who
had important stories to share with the world—they
could not exist without each other. Millennia later,

they were reunited. A joyful reunion. A meeting of the minds. They knew they knew each other. We knew we knew each other. That can be the only reason you were able to take the words right out of my heart and put them on paper. May the world celebrate our partnership; even better, may the people of the world experience such an incredible relationship.

THE family of READERS THAT I HAVE NOT yET MET

Love, in effortless abandon.

Reference Material and Further Reading

The history surrounding my story, and the stories of so many.

CHINA

- 1894–1895 First Sino-Japanese War.
- 1912 Republic of China replaces the Qing Dynasty.
- 1913–1927 An era of political instability due to infighting among warlords.
- 1914–1918 Japan enters World War I on the side of the Allies, hoping to increase its influence in Asia.
- 1927 Chiang Kai-shek stabilizes China.
- 1931 Japanese forces occupy Manchuria (this is the northeastern part of China and would not directly affect people in Guangzhou, which is west-northwest of Hong Kong).

My family was not in the part of China where the Japanese invaded (they were in Guangzhou), but the fact the Japanese did invade could have affected the decisions of my family of origin. After all, if Japan could be an aggressor in one part of China, why not others? Certainly, at that time, Japanese militarism was growing.

- My father's parents, born around 1910, walked out of China in the early 1930s—it is said they began in 1931. They would have been in their twenties. I've been told it was because of "war." It could have been a struggle for power between Nationalists, Communists, and warlords, and it could have been due to a steep decline in prices if their family's incomes were tied to the agricultural sector.

- The world depression hits China in the 1930s, with agricultural imports forcing down prices to desperate levels.

- 1937 Second invasion by Japanese through Shanghai (so farther south than my family's place of origin) and then in 1938 attacks on Chinese ports to prevent supplies of arms reaching the defenders. Aid from the USSR and the United States.

- In 1937, my grandparents would have been in Vietnam. Even if they had wanted to return to a more stable China, at that point, they could not have done so. The world was at war shortly after.

VIETNAM UP TO 1941

- Vietnam had been annexed by China in the second millennium BC.
- First independent monarch in the tenth century AD.
- The mid-nineteenth century saw European colonization (French—the area then called Indochina).
- When my grandparents arrived in Vietnam in the early 1930s, the French were exploiting the peasants and workers in general, with no regard for conditions or pay. Workers numbering over 100,000 were employed in mines and other industries, such as rubber.
- 1930 The Tonkin Mutiny, resisting French rule. There arose a privileged Vietnamese class, together with Chinese descendants, as middlemen and controllers of businesses, apart from big business controlled by the French. Forced labour was used for public works. Prior to World War II, 50 percent of the Vietnamese population did not own land.
- 1930 Vietnamese Communist Party was born.
- 1939 Population 20–23 million.
- 1939 About 15 percent of children received schooling—80 percent of the population was illiterate. There were only two doctors per 100,000 people compared to seventy-six per 100,000 in Japan.
- 1941 Japanese invasion. Vichy French government set up as puppet government.

VIETNAM BEYOND 1941

- Japanese soldiers stationed and directed to cut off supplies to China.
- After 1945, France tried to regain dominance in the area, which led, in 1946, to an insurgency by Viet Minh (organized in 1941, led by Hồ Chi Minh), translated to "League for the independence of Vietnam," put together to drive out the Japanese and French.
- 1950 Viet Minh and Chinese troops attack French outposts.
- The United States supports the French to stem communism.
- 1954 The French are defeated, and the Geneva Convention divides North and South. This was a decision by the victors of World War II, who believed Vietnam could not rule itself. This produced a split economy—agriculture in the South, industry in the North, a result of prior French economic development decisions.
- 1959 Civil war starts, the North attacking the South.
- The United States becomes involved in the conflict between North and South, initially in an advisory capacity.
- U.S. airstrikes on North Vietnam begin in early 1965.
- U.S. troop numbers—boots on the ground—peaked at 549,400 in 1968.
- 1969 onward—my parents grow a family.

- My grandparents' business becomes more successful by selling clothing to U.S. soldiers.
- 1973 U.S. withdrawal from Vietnam through the Paris Peace Accord.
- 1975 Saigon falls to the North Vietnamese.
- 1975 Grandfather's money and possessions are confiscated.
- 1976 The country is united as the Socialist Republic of Vietnam.
- The economy experiences a huge downturn. It is plagued by enormous difficulties in production, imbalance in supply and demand, inefficiencies in distribution and circulation, soaring inflation, rising debt problems, government corruption, and illegal asset confiscation.
- 1977 My grandparents are sponsored to go to Hong Kong.
- 1979 My parents fled with me and my five siblings.

THE AWARD: GRATITUDE FOR CANADA FROM THE WORLD

The Nansen Refugee Award is a medal issued annually by the United Nations High Commissioner for Refugees. It is usually awarded to an individual, group, or organization, in recognition of outstanding service to the cause of refugees and displaced or stateless people. However, on February 18, 1986, the Nansen Medal was awarded to an entire nation. That nation was Canada. At that time, the High Commissioner was Jean-Pierre Hocké, who presented the award and spoke about the contributions Canada had made.

Canada was recognized as a country that successfully resettled refugees in every province and territory.

The United Nations praised the exemplary humanitarian effort put forward by a country whose geography is diverse and whose regions are massive, and whose population is relatively small compared to its land size. It was a testament to its commitment to serve the world, as it had for decades with its famous blue-bereted peacekeepers.

The United Nations High Commission recognized the compassion of Canada's response and acknowledged the many sectors that had come together to respond to such a crisis. The speeches mentioned how Canada worked hard to alleviate myriad difficult situations for refugees around the world.

It was the first and only time that this prestigious medal has been awarded to an entire nation.

About the Author

Dr. Vi Tu Banh is a living, breathing part of the diversity of Canada. He graciously serves patients in his Uxbridge, Ontario, optometry clinic, where he has become renowned for healing balance issues, stabilizing the effects of concussions, and addressing learning challenges by using state-of-the-art technology and current vision therapy techniques. Visit uxbridgeoptometry.com to learn more. He lives nearby with his soulmate, Mamie. Invested in exploring higher consciousness, he is a philanthropist who enjoys an active physical life. His first book is *12 Elephants and a Dragon*.

ABOUT MARIE BESWICK ARTHUR

Marie has long believed we are all infinite story. She writes to change the world. Her imagination changes ideas into art, and her ability to understand the voices of others allows her to bring their stories to life.

Marie brings a unique aspect to the projects she mastercrafts. In the beginning, Marie wrote over 200 Lifebooks for Children's Services in Alberta, Canada. These truthful narratives in story form helped children in the system come to terms with why they were removed from their biological parents. Over the last thirty years, Marie has collaborated on more than fifty published books, some of which are award-winning. For her solo work, she has received awards for poetry and short stories. Her debut novel, *Listen for Water*, published in 2022, received the 2022 Titan Literary Gold Award. Future works are forthcoming. She mentors and writes from her heart, which is flexibly and lovingly attached to Mexico, Canada, and the UK.

www.ingramcontent.com/pod-product-compliance
Lightning Source LLC
Chambersburg PA
CBHW031458120626
46545CB00005B/1656